Local Food, Local Restaurants, Local Recipes

The MINNESOTA HOMEGROWN COOKBOOK

Presented by Renewing the Countryside

FOREWORD BY GARRISON KEILLOR

Voyageur Press

For our friend, mentor, and unbeatable dinner companion, Dick Broeker

First published in 2008 by Voyageur Press, an imprint of MBI Publishing Company LLC, 400 First Avenue North, Suite 300, Minneapolis, MN 55401 USA

Voyageur Press titles are also available at discounts in bulk quantity for industrial or sales-promotional use. For details write to Special Sales Manager at MBI Publishing Company, 400 First Avenue North, Suite 300, Minneapolis, MN 55401 USA.

To find out more about our books, join us online at www.voyageurpress.com.

Voyageur Press Editor: Michael Dregni

A Renewing the Countryside Project
2637 27th Avenue South, Minneapolis, MN 55406
1-866-477-1521 • www.renewingthecountryside.org

Support for this project provided through a grant from North Central Region Sustainable Agriculture Research and Education
Project Director: Jan Joannides
Creative Director: Brett Olson
Editors: Alice Tanghe, Jan Joannides, and Stephanie Larson
Writers: Tim King and Alice Tanghe
Recipe Editors: Alice Tanghe and Mary Broeker
Senior Photographer: Anthony Brett Schreck
Photographers: Brett Olson, Kristi Link Fernholz, John Connelly, Richard Hamilton Smith, and Dave Holman
Advisory Committee: Mary Broeker, Jan Joannides, Tim King, Chuck Knierim, Brett Olson, and Alice Tanghe
Project Assistants: Beth Munnich, Andi McDaniel, Derric Pennington, Margaret Schnieders, and Sarah Johnson

Library of Congress Cataloging-in-Publication Data

Renewing the Countryside (Organization)
    The Minnesota homegrown cookbook : local food, local restaurants,
local recipes / [compiled by Renewing the Countryside]. —1st ed.
    p. cm.
  Includes index.
  "A Renewing the Countryside project."
  ISBN-13: 978-0-7603-3142-2 (hb w/ jacket)
  ISBN-10: 0-7603-3142-1 (hb w/ jacket)
    1. Cookery (Natural foods)   2. Cookery,—Minnesota.
3. Restaurants—Minnesota—Guidebooks. 4. Sustainable
agriculture—Minnesota. I. Title.
TX741.R458 2008
641.59776—dc22
                                    2007049718

Printed in China

CONTENTS

FOREWORD

BY GARRISON KEILLOR

I grew up a few steps from a half-acre vegetable garden, and it pretty much ruined me for fine dining forever after. When you've eaten sweet corn ten minutes removed from the stalk, you've experienced intense sensual pleasure at a young age, and what can the great chefs of New York and Paris offer to compete with it?

My father John loved sweet corn and most other fresh vegetables, also raspberries and strawberries, and after Christmas he pored over the seed catalogues with all the varieties with names like race horses: Contender, Kentucky Wonder, Little Marvel, Early Perfection, Silver Queen, Early Prolific, and I recall a broccoli called the Brigadier. And also Detroit Supreme Beets. He was a Minnesota farm boy, and even after we moved to the outskirts of Minneapolis, he preferred to butcher his own chickens rather than buy the plastic-wrapped stuff at Super Valu. In the spring, he plowed the half acre and planted the rows — the strawberry beds and raspberry patch lay to the east so he planted melons and cucumbers on the west side of the plot, a regiment of corn to the rear, the pole beans and tomatoes and peas and root crops in the middle — and as we ate the last Mason jars of Mother's canned goods from the shelves in the laundry room and cleaned out the freezer, we awaited the glories of July and August and September.

In sweet corn season, Mother fixed Sunday dinner or weekday supper, got the pot roast or meatloaf or hot dish all set, and had a big pot of water boiling on the stove before we kids were dispatched to pick the corn. We picked an armload and started husking it as we walked to the house and put the naked ears in the boiling water for a few minutes, the prayer was said, the platter of steaming corn on the cob was brought to the table, we distributed it with tongs and slathered it with butter and salted it and ate it in our hands, chewing the kernels off either in lateral or circular fashion, and we never ever said, "This sure is good sweet corn!" Never. You'd only say that if somebody served you week-old storebought corn, to make them feel better. The ten-minute corn was beyond goodness — it was a spiritual experience, proof that God exists and that He loves you, and there is no need to compliment God on the sweet corn, what's necessary is to love this gift and enjoy it, and we did.

There were six of us children, so labor was cheap, and the soil was good black loam, and the output of that half-acre was just prodigious. Awesome, in fact. The gross yield of forty tomato plants can give you daily salads, bushels of tomatoes to stew and can, and bags of tomatoes to take to relatives in the city. But the greatest prize is for the boy hoeing the tomatoes

who reaches down and rescues one and wipes the dust off and bites into it. That is pure pleasure, a privilege offered to few, and after it, you will never be happy with any tomato you buy in a store. You hold it to your nose and there is no tomatoness there whatsoever. It was bred for shelf life and strip-mined in Mexico, or the Imperial Valley of California, and artificially ripened, and now it has no more tomato essence than your shoe. This is why vinaigrette dressing was invented: to provide some flavor for denatured vegetables.

Where I grew up in the late forties and fifties, in Brooklyn Park township along the Mississippi five miles north of the Minneapolis city limits, there were truck farms — "truck" here means "miscellany," not the motorized vehicle — that raised vegetables for sale at the farmers market near downtown. There was a farm that specialized in radishes and onions and another that mostly raised strawberries. The Fishers had a big asparagus operation, and Fred Peterson raised sweet corn and peas, and there were potato farms north of us along the West River Road and over towards Osseo. A boy could hop on his bike and ride off any summer morning and find work there, put in eight hours picking potatoes and earn fifty cents an hour plus a bag of unsellable scabby potatoes to take home for supper.

My family was in the first wave of settlement after World War II. My dad got a G.I. loan to buy lumber, and he built the house himself on an acre of cornfield he bought from Fred Peterson, and other houses sprang up near us, and all of them had big vegetable gardens. That was the beauty of the acre lot: you put a house and yard on half of it and farmed the other half. When the value of land zoomed in the late sixties, people sold off that back half-acre. It was ironical — the urge to have some land on which to raise a garden led to a land rush that wiped out the gardens — and soon the lovers of sweet corn and tomatoes had to settle far from the city and endure long commutes.

And most of us children who grew up on fresh tomatoes went off to live lives that did not include a garden. All but one of my father's siblings — Lawrence, Jim, Eleanor, Elizabeth, Bob, Josephine — had vegetable gardens of considerable breadth and variety, and none of my five siblings raise their own food and neither do I. We all became city dwellers and had better things to do with our time. We went to the movies. We stayed late at the office. We dashed from home to a meeting and then back to the office and en route, hungry, we saw the golden arches and drove up to the intercom and got the burger and fries and ate it as we drove. There was no McTomato or McCorn on the menu.

The co-op movement of the seventies placed a premium on Local and Organic, and that has led us back toward the garden. In my neighborhood co-op I can occasionally find tomatoes that smell of tomato, and if I drive over to Wisconsin in the summer I will eventually find a pickup truck parked by a field and a big sign SWEET CORN and a boy sitting in the shade. And if my wife and I go to the right restaurant, we will find a menu that tells where the salad comes from and where the fish was caught and who raised the cow who provided the strip steak, which is always of interest.

I can never be a boy again standing barefoot in a garden on a sunny day and holding a ripe tomato in my hand — don't really want to be him anyway — but this lovely book gives me hope that something beautiful that I thought had passed away has actually come full circle and that other people in Minnesota share this same longing for fresh food. Back in my childhood, the Sunday paper sometimes ran stories about What the World Will Be Like In the Year 2000 and, in addition to travel by rocket cars and living in glass-domed houses, the futurists agreed that people in 2000 would take their meals in the form of pills. This did not strike us as something to look forward to. The futurists were thinking only of convenience — we are a restless people and notoriously impatient and so you might assume that we'd prefer to have dinner in the form of capsules, gulp them down, save ourselves the trouble — but in fact we have a secret longing for pleasure, too. We are some of the hardest-working people on the planet, and we deserve a little reward now and then. A fresh tomato, sliced, with chilled cucumber and pepper and onion. An ear of corn. Six small red potatoes, boiled in their skins. All of it homegrown. From this, one can regain faith in divine providence and restore a sense of the kindness and beauty of the world and resolve to rise up tomorrow and try to do what needs to be done.

INTRODUCTION

All food is not created equal. Anyone who bites into a just-picked tomato on a warm summer day knows that it hardly resembles that tomato-like thing you get in Minnesota grocery stores in January. And cheese crafted by an artisan cheesemaker is worlds apart from those single-wrapped, processed slices that many of us grew up on.

This is a book about homegrown food. Not necessarily homegrown, as in your own garden, but homegrown by farmers and producers across the state.

In this book we take you on a journey. It begins on the North Shore and traverses the state, covering the Red River Valley, Minnesota River Valley, Pine and Lakes Country, Bluff Country, and the Twin Cities. It delves into the interdependent relationships between farmers and chefs, between local ingredients and good food.

We share the stories of chefs and cooks who are passionate about local foods. They know that food raised by local farmers is fresher and tastes better than food that travels across the country—or the world. They willingly adjust their menus to incorporate the freshest local ingredients. Seasonality is something they embrace.

The farmers we visit are equally as passionate about the food they produce. They use innovative and sustainable techniques to raise the best food and raise it in a way that cares for the environment. They are concerned about treating their animals humanely and about delivering a product that is healthy for those who eat it.

In addition to farmers, we visit food gatherers who skillfully tap maple trees, fish Lake Superior, or harvest wild rice. We also meet artisan foodmakers who create a mouthwatering array of cheeses, wines, jams, and other tasty morsels.

Tucked among the stories are an array of tantalizing recipes from the chefs and cooks featured. They demonstrate what can be created from the fresh, seasonal food we have locally.

As you make your way through the stories and recipes, you may not even notice that there are no bay scallops or basmati rice recipes. Oh sure, you'll find recipes with chocolate and lemons, but you'll also be surprised by the rich and amazingly diverse palate showcased here, from corn chowder to morel mushroom, goat cheese, and asparagus fettuccine.

The chefs and farmers featured here are just a fraction of the growing number who are changing the way we think about food. We're in the midst of a local foods revolution. It tastes better. It's healthier. And it's better for the planet.

We don't suggest you give up oranges, coffee, or chocolate, but protest a little when someone tries to sell you an apple from New Zealand in October. French and California wines are great, but try one of the new Minnesota wines. Plant a tomato, visit a farmers' market, join a CSA or a food co-op. Ask your favorite grocery store, restaurant, local hospital, or your child's school if they buy locally grown food. If they don't, encourage them to do so. This isn't about being fanatical but rather about using common sense—the sense that tells you when something tastes good and is good for you and your community.

Eat locally grown food because it is fresh. Eat locally grown food because it is healthy. Eat it because you care about supporting a sustainable, healthy countryside and because you want small farms to continue to be viable. Eat locally grown food because you can.

Enjoy!

NORTH SHORE

ANGRY TROUT CAFE

Dockside Fish Market

The *Angry Trout Cafe Notebook* is dedicated to Marybeth and Martha, George Wilkes' children. The dedication reads, "May the failings of my generation lead to the awakening of yours."

George is the co-owner and co-founder of the Angry Trout Cafe in Grand Marais, along with his wife, Barb LaVigne. He wrote the book as a way to explain to Angry Trout's customers, friends, the world, and perhaps himself, his deepening and broadening thinking about sustainability and where his little cafe at the end of the pier on the edge of a big cold lake fits into a larger picture. He subtitled his book *Friends, Recipes, and the Culture of Sustainability.*

Barb LaVigne and George Wilkes

George writes, "I like to think of the success of our cafe as being dependent on the amount of meaning that our customers experience. On a basic level, good food and service at an acceptable price is the standard measure when going out to eat — but what if that delicious swordfish dinner contributes to the decline of the Atlantic swordfish population?"

Given two restaurants of equal quality, George believes customers will choose the one with the better stories. He contends, "Sustainability is a powerful story."

"What George and Barb are doing is great — and it's working," says Shele Toftey, whose family supplies the Angry Trout with fresh and smoked fish from Lake Superior. "That's what's amazing. It seems like each year they get more into it." What

George and Barb are getting into, in part, is forming strong bonds with the residents of the lakeside community of Grand Marais.

Those bonds have built understanding and trust that transcends the occasional petty differences that can arise between neighbors. Shele's had some differences with George over a few of his ideas about sustainability, but she acknowledges that everyone is welcome to his or her opinion. Besides, she values the fact that she can walk the thirty feet or so from her family's Dockside Fish Market to the Angry Trout Cafe to borrow a head of lettuce if she runs out.

Relationships that allow borrowing lettuce from your neighbor may be one thing George had in mind when he used the term "culture of sustainability" in the subtitle of his book.

For their part, George and Barb prize the fact that they can see Toftey's fishing boat coming off Lake Superior most summer mornings with the day's herring catch. They know that the fish they'll be serving their customers will be only hours old. They also know that it takes dedicated and rugged individuals to head out onto the lake at daylight to gillnet herring. Gillnetting is a fishing technique brought to the area by Scandinavian immigrants. It is an art form that requires skill and endurance in nice weather, and the weather on the big lake isn't always nice.

Then there is the excellent customer service. "Every morning I look in their cooler and I pretty much know what they go through," Shele says. "We almost always get it right, and they have fresh fish on hand. The few times they've run out, they just walk over and let us know. We can get it over there in two minutes."

The identity of the Angry Trout Cafe, along with its famous fish 'n chips and grilled Lake Superior fish of the day, is linked to the Toftey's and that, in turn, to Lake Superior's waters, people, and history. That can make for some pretty interesting fish stories. Stories like how Shele grew up on Oregon's Pacific coast and used to fish the long line boats of Alaska for halibut and black cod. Stories about how Shele met Harley in Alaska while they were fishing for salmon, and how they married and came back to an inland sea.

When the herring season on Lake Superior closes during November spawning, the Toftey's go inland to Greenwood Lake. There, for a few weeks before it ices up, they net lake herring and whitefish. Some of the whitefish served at the Angry Trout comes from the Tofteys, but that's most likely smoked. That's because when the Tofteys are netting whitefish in November, the Angry Trout is closed for the season.

The rare treat of fresh whitefish that sometimes shows up on the menu at the Angry Trout Cafe likely came from members of the Grand Portage Band of Ojibwe. They are the only commercial fishermen who can set nets for fish other than herring in Lake Superior because of their treaty rights. "If you ever see fresh whitefish on the specials board, order it right away because it won't be there very long!" George advises.

A visit to the Angry Trout spawns many questions. Who made the beautiful carving of the blue herons on the door to the cafe? Why are the organic cotton napkins so small? Where were these plates made? Who raised the delicious pork you can now find on the menu? Do they make that delicious sourdough bread right here? And why is the trout so angry?

There are some answers at hand. The answer to the last question is provided by Ms. Elaine Fisch, renowned medium to the spirit world and founder of the Society for the Prevention of Cruelty to Crystals, on page two of *The Angry Trout Cafe Notebook*. As for the sourdough bread, Toni Mason — of Grand Marais' own Good Harbor Hill Bread Company — baked it.

George and Barb are pleased to serve Toni's bread. And they're pleased a local woodworker made the chairs for the cafe and another local, Kimball Creek Woodworks, crafted the salt-shakers and pepper mills. By supporting local artisans who make products from renewable resources and farmers who grow food organically, George and Barb hope they are helping to build a better world for their daughters.

Meanwhile, Shele Toftey is wondering if her nine-year-old twins will someday be interested in fishing, or running the Dockside Fish Market. "There are so many things to get kids' attention now; you never know what will happen," she says, "but it would be wonderful if when they got older, they wanted to fish with us."

As a businesswoman, Shele is impressed with George and Barb's success. As a mother, she may be wondering if in their work lies the seed of possibility that her daughters will carry on the Toftey tradition. "We've always been fishermen," she says. "The Toftey family were fishermen in Norway before they came to Lake Superior."

For her daughters' sake, she hopes that George and Barb, as well as she and Harley, can get more things right than wrong.

Shele Tofte and a smoked herring at the Dockside Fish Market

Harley Tofte, left, fishing on Lake Superior

WILD MUSHROOM-TOMATO BISQUE

Serves 4

$^1/_2$ cup sliced leek

$^1/_4$ cup minced shallot

1 stalk celery, chopped

1 teaspoon dried dill

2 tablespoons butter

2 cups sliced fresh shiitake mushrooms

1 16-ounce can crushed tomatoes

$1^1/_2$ cups vegetable stock

Salt and white pepper to taste

$^1/_2$ cup heavy cream

1 clove garlic, minced

$^1/_2$ cup additional fresh sliced mushrooms

$^1/_4$ cup chopped fresh dill

Heat butter in a large pot, and sauté leek, shallot, celery, and dill for about 4 minutes. Add mushrooms and sauté until tender. Add tomatoes, stock, salt, and pepper, and bring to a boil. Reduce heat, cover, and simmer for 20 minutes.

Add cream and garlic. Using an immersion blender (or a regular blender), blend soup until smooth. Heat throughly and check seasoning.

For garnish: sauté an additional $^1/_2$ cup of sliced mushrooms in butter. Place sautéed mushroom slices on top of soup with chopped fresh dill.

SMOKED HERRING WITH CRANBERRY HORSERADISH SAUCE

$^1/_2$ cup sour cream

$^1/_4$ cup sugar

1 tablespoon horseradish

$1^1/_4$ cups fresh or frozen cranberries

2 tablespoons minced red onion

Smoked herring and/or smoked, de-boned trout

Slices of French bread

In a bowl, mix sour cream, sugar, and horseradish. In a blender or food processor, blend cranberries and onion to a slightly chunky consistency. Do not liquefy. Add cranberry-onion blend to sour cream mixture and mix. Refrigerate for a while to blend the flavors.

Serve with whole smoked herring or de-boned smoked trout and slices of baguette.

BLUEBERRY CREAM TART

By Misha Martin, available at Angry Trout or at Misha Martin's Sweets

CRUST
¾ cup unsalted butter
½ cup powdered sugar
2 cups all-purpose flour

Preheat oven to 300°F. Cream the butter in a mixer bowl on medium. Turn to low, and add flour and sugar. Mix until just mixed and crumbly. Press into an 11-inch tart pan with removable bottom. Bake for 15 to 20 minutes until slightly golden. Cool on rack.

FILLING
8 ounces cream cheese, at room temperature
½ cup sour cream
½ cup powdered sugar

In mixer bowl, cream the softened cream cheese. Add sugar and sour cream, and blend on medium until smooth and fluffy. Pour into cooled tart shell and smooth top. Refrigerate.

BERRY LAYER
3 cups fresh blueberries, cleaned
1 cup sugar
1 cup water

Put berries in a strainer over a pan. Simmer sugar and water together in a saucepan for 1 minute. Take off heat and pour over berries immediately. Toss berries slightly in strainer.

Take syrup from the catch pan under the berries and pour over berries once more, with the saucepan as the catchpan. Drain berries completely and distribute over top of refrigerated filling. They will be a little sticky and hold together nicely. Refrigerate until served.

Remaining liquid can be boiled down and used as syrup with pancakes or ice cream, or can be mixed with soda water to make a blueberry soda.

CHEZ JUDE

Wild Acres Game Farm

A winter's full moon, lifting above Lake Superior's wintry waters, is a cheering sight. Dining at Chez Jude in Grand Marais, during the restaurant's full moon dining weeks, blends the grand drama of moonrise with the intimacy of Chef Judi Barsness' North Shore cuisine. The gentle clink of china and silver, a glowing fireplace, an artfully presented plate, and the blue shimmer of moonbeam are most restorative.

"In the winter we are open for one week a month, during the full moon," Judi explains. "The other weeks we run our cooking school, which operates only in winter."

At other times of the year, Chez Jude is open for all phases of the moon — for lunch, afternoon tea, dinner, and late-night dining. The menu changes weekly in order to use the freshest ingredients of the seasons and the local harvest.

Chez Jude's full moon dining, afternoon tea, and cooking school ought to signal that a unique culinary experience is happening in this little harbor town on the big lake. It is, of course, Judi. As the chef and owner, Chez Jude is her expression. But Judi is quick to note: "Chez Jude is not just me. The talented people that work with me everyday help make what we do happen on a grand level. I am so lucky to have a great team."

Judi, a second-generation chef, also credits her French mother for her success. It was in her restaurant kitchen that Judi's skills and passion for cooking were first learned. The

Judi Barsness

Culinary Institute of America, Greystone; the National Baking Center; her internship at Alice Waters' restaurant, Chez Panisse; Full Belly Organic Farm, where she first experienced the full meaning of "farm to table"; and most certainly the farmers, fishermen, ranchers, and cheese artisans she buys from have all had an effect on what you experience at Chez Jude.

On an October evening, Judi can be found making her mother's recipe of boneless short ribs of beef Bourguignon à la Marie Louise, using cultivated and wild mushrooms from Forest Mushrooms in St. Joseph. "The short ribs came from Thousand Hills Cattle Company and the fresh baby carrots and rutabaga came through the local food co-op in Grand Marais," she says, over the rumble of the kitchen exhaust fans. "I'm serving that over an organic root vegetable and golden potato mousse, which I'll garnish with a horseradish crème fraîche."

The finished dish will be topped with a sprinkle of herbs, and perhaps fresh flowers from the Chez Jude kitchen garden. "Edible flowers, so fresh the bees just visited them," are important to Judi. That is why the restaurant has a kitchen garden and why Judi celebrates the local and regional farmers with whose food she cooks. Local products like herbs from Kim Falter's Wild Edible Gardens, Sonja Helland's wild rice, Herb Wills' Caribou Cream maple syrup, and Good Harbor Hill Bread Company assure a freshness and taste not available in the back of a restaurant supply truck coming up from Duluth or the Twin Cities.

Community is important to Judi. On the back of the menu is her "I get by with a little help from my friends" list. Local and regional suppliers, like Cook County Whole Foods Cooperative, can be found in the moon shadows of the restaurant. Grand Marais is, agriculturally speaking, Minnesota's Last Chance Saloon. The seasons are short, the rocks are hard, and the winters are long. But friends can help overcome those challenges.

"I often partner with the co-op when we get into our slower season," Judi says. "Because I'm just a small chef-owned restaurant, I sometimes can't hit the large minimums required by organic wholesalers. So we partner with the co-op on a delivery."

But there's more to it than that. "What is really neat about partnering with my local co-op is that when our customers taste a new flavor, we can tell them to go right over to the Cook County Co-op and get the ingredient," Judi says. "Last week I made a pumpkin and apple soup that used maple syrup. I was able to tell people where to find the sugar pumpkins, Haralson apples, and Caribou Cream maple syrup."

"Freshness is the key," Judi adds. "When you're dealing with local suppliers, you're getting the freshest food you can possibly get. That freshness, and the sustainable manner in which the food was raised or harvested, provides an enhanced flavor. Real food with real flavor." On another level, Judi knows that she is not only supporting local growers, but also supporting sustainability of the environment and the economy where she lives. She says, "It's like a big circle. We all support each other. This is all very important to me as a chef, as a business person, and as a citizen of not only my community, but of my planet."

When you walk through Chez Jude's red door, you enter this circle of "friends" and happily link yourself to the food chain. Go to an elegant afternoon tea, for instance. Should you

Rene Swadburg

order the English High Tea or North Shore Afternoon Tea? The latter features local northern artisan cheeses, such as Eichten's Wild Rice Gouda, Shepherd's Way Big Woods Blue, Carr Valley's Benedictine and Mobay; Lake Superior caviar and smoked fish from local fisherman, Harley Toftey; olives, flat breads, and a toasted-nut chocolate-chip tart with bittersweet chocolate drizzle. English High Tea features mango chicken hazelnut salad finger sandwiches; cream tea scones, butter, jam, and lemon curd; and vanilla bean cheesecake with raspberry coulis.

"To make the finger sandwiches, we chop some roasted chicken breast with mango, toasted hazelnuts, and tarragon caper aioli," Judi explains, "and put that on our own orange currant brioche with cucumber, organic greens, and herbed boursin cheese."

Chicken comes to Chez Jude from Beaver Creek Farm in Wisconsin or Wild Acres Game Farm in Pequot Lakes. Pat Ebnet of Wild Acres attends the same church of freshness that Judi does. "I process it one day and it's in the restaurants or meat markets the next day," Pat says.

Wild Acres, which produces not only chicken but also turkey, pheasant, quail, and duck, is large for a family-run poultry farm. They process about 50,000 birds annually by employing three full-time and up to fourteen part-time employees. Pat says the full-time employees, who are long-term, have become more like family members. And when his two young children want to turn the eggs in the hatchery or help on processing day, they do. "Sometimes they ride with me on delivery day," Pat says. "They like to help with invoicing. They know all the chefs and who to ask for a chocolate chip cookie."

So if you are dining in the moonlight on Chez Jude's Wood Roasted Bistro Chicken, think of the Ebnet children — and all the farmers, bakers, and gatherers — who are links in this local circle of friends and food providers.

BISTRO ROASTED CHICKEN

The high temperatures and local maple and applewood smoke from the Chez Jude wood-fired oven create the unique flavor and crispy seasoned skin of this Bistro Chicken. Judi varies this dish seasonally by adding diced butternut squash to the onion sauté stage in the fall. Using the same wine that will accompany the meal will create the best flavor.

½ lb. applewood smoked bacon, cut in small pieces
A 3 to 4-lb. free-range chicken (from Wild Acres), quartered and rubbed with Chez Jude Herbs de Provence (recipe below)
1 cup chopped onion
3 tablespoons unbleached organic all-purpose flour
3 cups red wine; a burgundy is the traditional choice. Do not use a wine that is very fruity.
3 cups chicken stock or organic broth
2 tablespoons tomato paste
1 tablespoon fresh rosemary, chopped
1 cup baby green top carrots
2 cups pearl onions, blanched and skinned (or use frozen)
2 cups fresh mushrooms, shiitake, and crimini, quartered
2 tablespoons red currant jelly
2 tablespoons fresh chopped Italian parsley
Salt and pepper to taste

In a brasier or Dutch oven, sauté the bacon until crisp, remove with a slotted spoon and drain on paper towels. Set aside. Pour off all but 2 tablespoons of the bacon drippings.

Brown the chicken in the drippings, on both sides, over medium high heat. Remove the chicken and place into a roasting pan in a 400°F wood-fired or conventional oven. Roast for an additional 30 minutes or about ⅔ of the way done. Don't overcook; you will be reheating the chicken at a later time. Cover and store in the refrigerator until you are ready for the final preparation. Chicken can be stored at this point up to 2 days.

Note: Add any roasting juices into the braiser or Dutch oven. Do not forget to scrape up the browned bits and add these into your stew pot; they add another layer of rich flavor. Then, make the vegetable stew.

To make the vegetable stew, add the chopped onions to the pan that was used to brown the chicken; sprinkle with salt, pepper, and the flour. Stir constantly, and continue to cook for 5 minutes. This will "cook" the flour and remove the starchy taste. This also aids in thickening the stew in the simmer reduction stage of cooking. Add the wine, stock, tomato paste, crisp bacon, and rosemary; bring to a boil. Add carrots, pearl onions, and mushrooms. Cover the pot and turn down the heat to medium low or simmer. Continue to cook until the vegetables are cooked through. You can remove the cover and cook until the sauce is reduced or thickened if needed.

Add the red currant jelly and parsley, to heat through. Taste and adjust seasoning as needed. This stew can be prepared up to 2 days prior to serving.

On the day of serving. Prepare the Yukon Gold and Root Vegetable Mousse (recipe page 23). When ready to plate, reheat the chicken in a 350°F oven for 15 minutes. Bring the vegetable stew up to serving temperature. Place the roasted chicken in a large rimmed bowl upon a nest of root vegetable and potato mousse (or soft polenta or cooked egg noodles). Ladle the red wine stew of vegetables over the chicken. Garnish with a drizzle of crème fraîche and a sprig of fresh rosemary. Serve with crusty bread and butter.

HERBS DE PROVENCE MEAT RUB

Use for meats, wild game, or poultry.

1 cup olive oil
3 tablespoons minced garlic
3 tablespoons herbs de Provence (dried mixture of thyme, rosemary, sage, lavender, basil, fennel seed, marjoram, summer savory, available in the spice section of your local grocery)
Fresh cracked black pepper and kosher salt, to taste

Whisk all ingredients together. Rub on meats and let marinate for 2 hours prior to cooking.

YUKON GOLD AND ROOT VEGETABLE MOUSSE

This is a potato dish that will become a favorite.

2 lbs. Yukon gold potatoes, peeled and quartered
$\frac{1}{4}$ lb. parsnips, peeled and diced $\frac{1}{4}$ inch
$\frac{1}{4}$ small rutabaga, peeled and shredded
2 minced garlic cloves
$\frac{1}{4}$ cup butter
1 green onion, chopped
$\frac{1}{2}$ cup sour cream or crème fraîche
Fresh chopped Italian parsley, salt and pepper to taste

Boil the potatoes, parsnips, rutabaga, and minced garlic cloves together, about 20 minutes or until tender but not mushy. Drain and return to the pan to dry over low heat.

Place in mixer outfitted with a paddle, add butter, and mix on low speed until the butter is melted. Add the remaining ingredients and continue to mix on low speed until the desired texture is achieved, from slightly chunky to smooth. Taste and adjust seasoning before serving.

WILD BLUEBERRY MAPLE CRÈME BRÛLÉE

A great dessert to serve after a hearty stew. Judi uses heavy cream from Cedar Summit, locally harvested maple syrup from Caribou Cream Maple Syrup, and blueberries that she and her forager/CSA friends harvest from their woodland properties on the North Shore, or organic berries purchased through the local Whole Foods Cooperative.

2 cups heavy cream
$\frac{1}{2}$ whole vanilla bean, scraped (or 2 teaspoons pure vanilla)
1 egg
3 large egg yolks
7 tablespoons real maple syrup
6 tablespoons small wild blueberries (fresh or frozen)
4 tablespoons turbinado sugar (raw sugar)
Four 8 oz. ramekins

Preheat oven to 325°F. Scald the heavy cream with halved and scraped vanilla bean (or use pure liquid vanilla). In mixing bowl, combine the whole egg, yolks, and maple syrup until well mixed. Temper the egg mixture by adding one third of the hot cream into the eggs while whisking constantly. Add remaining hot cream and mix. (Tempering the egg mixture prevents the eggs from turning into scrambled eggs!) Strain the mixture, removing the vanilla bean.

Place about 1 tablespoon of blueberries into the ramekins. Fill half full with the custard. Add a few additional blueberries, and fill ramekins with custard.

Set the ramekins in a baking pan; fill baking pan with boiling water halfway up the sides of the ramekins. Bake until set, approximately 40 minutes.

Remove ramekins from the water bath and let cool before covering and storing. Refrigerate 8 hours prior to serving. Can be stored up to 2 to 3 days.

Blot any moisture that is on the top of the ramekins. Sprinkle turbinado raw sugar or maple sugar on the custard, caramelize with a chef's torch or under the broiler.

Top left: Pat Ebnet and chicks

ELLERY HOUSE BED AND BREAKFAST

Park Lake Farm

Joan and Jim Halquist

Winter is long and serene in northern Minnesota. There is time for the snow to softly accumulate. To ski. To lay another log on the fire . . . and another. To sleep in. Spring is a long way off. It may not even come this year.

In winter's grip, this would seem true to all but those few who are truly in tune. They hear the owls in January, the great grey and great horned, hooting and frolicking. They are aware of stirrings.

In February, the eelpout — the most Minnesotan of fish — migrate and mate under lifeless ice. It is then that Joel Rosen stirs. He feels it. He hears it. And in the depths of winter's already faltering clutch, Joel begins his Park Lake Farm garden near Mahtowa.

Don't despair if you can't visit Joel until early March; he'll still have time to visit. Maybe he'll share a cup of his notoriously muscular coffee, with a spot of syrup from his sugar bush. If you visit him in mid-March, you may locate him shearing sheep. He may tell you to brew your own coffee while his conversation is limited to a few scattered sentences. He may mention that he's delayed a few weeks on planting.

And, you may lean against the cold wall of the silent barn and hear the cutting of shears on thick, oily wool, hear Joel grunt as he lays the ewe down, bleating, and feel the hotness of the coffee in the back of your mouth.

Sheep shearing barely precedes maple syrup time at Park Lake Farm. There is often a story recounted that at time's beginning, maple sap, already viscous and sweet, dripped from trees. When the first people discovered this, they did what you and I would do — they lay down by the maples and drank syrup until they fell asleep. The creator came to look in on his creations, but he found the village empty and the cook fires cold. When he discovered the people lying under the maples, corpulent and soft, he stormed and raged about the sugar bush and set out to put things right. And now, as any Minnesotan who has spent time in the sugar bush can tell you, it takes about forty gallons of sap to make a gallon of syrup.

But the creator must have been distracted when he passed by Park Lake. "We have an average of about thirty gallons of sap to one gallon of syrup, and one year we were twenty to one," Joel says. "When it's twenty to one, it's half the work, half the firewood to make and stoke, and half the sap to lift." That translates to 1,200 fewer gallons of sap to haul and cook if you, like Joel has on occasion, make sixty gallons of syrup. With such a ratio, corpulence isn't far off.

"I used to think this stuff was expensive until I came out and helped Joel cook it," says Jim Halquist, who along with his wife Joan, is the owner of Duluth's Ellery House Bed and Breakfast.

Jim, who is a longtime friend and customer of Joel's, knows the truth about syrup in a way that transcends the mere telling. He's hauled the buckets, stoked the fires, and helped Joel finish a batch of syrup after it has come off Park Lake Farm's home-made sap evaporator.

"Jim and Joan buy about twenty-four quarts a year from us," Joel says. "They might like a little more, but I've only got so much. I like to make sure all my customers get some." So when the Halquists provide you with maple syrup for your Ellery House stuffed French toast, know that it is precious and rare.

Like their friend Joel, the Halquists take pleasure in providing the rarities. At their gracious breakfast table they serve good, nourishing fare and interesting conversation. When guests first enter Ellery House, they experience first the aroma, then the flavor of Joan's macadamia nut chocolate chip cookies.

Jim, a minister's son, thinks of his work as a sort of ministry as well. "My father took care of the needs of the soul," he says. "A lot of people who come here have had a physically and mentally trying week. A stay at Ellery House can soothe their tired body and mind."

A comfortable place with unpretentious elegance, Jim says, "It's a little like coming to your grandmother or great-aunt's house. It's a vision we have where keeping a house is a vocation.

It used to be an art. Nowadays, you go to Byerly's and buy the cookies or brownies. Here, we make them for you. We also make truffles. It's easy."

Yes, easy, like planting onions in February, shearing sheep in March, making syrup in April, and then lambing in May. And after lambing come planting, weeding, cultivating, harvesting, and selling. It is the routine annual madness that has brought joy to Joel Rosen these last twenty seasons at Park Lake Farm. And it is his abiding pleasure to share it with customers like Jim and Joan, who understand its origins and purpose. While his link with people like the Halquists provides another dimension to his life, Jim says the same is true for him. His life is deepened by his relationship with Joel and Park Lake Farm.

Whereas Joel's farm life circles out to reach Ellery House, life at the bed and breakfast is uniquely urban. The Victorian Ellery House is on the edge of a deep wooded ravine just two blocks from Lake Superior. There are raccoon, deer, and occasionally, a bear in the ravine. But the Halquists can serve their guests breakfast, made all the better with Joel's maple syrup, and be in the city for sailing by late morning.

"Owning Ellery House has allowed us to have the gift of living and raising our children in Duluth," Jim says. It is a gift that they take pleasure in sharing with their guests.

Joel Rosen

JOAN'S STRAWBERRY RHUBARB MUFFINS

Makes 12 muffins

1¾ cups flour
½ cup sugar
2½ teaspoons baking powder
¾ teaspoon salt
1 egg, slightly beaten
¾ cup plain yogurt (milk can be substituted)
⅓ cup vegetable oil
½ teaspoon vanilla
¾ cup diced fresh rhubarb
1 cup chopped fresh strawberries

Preheat oven to 400°F. In a large bowl, mix flour, sugar, baking powder, and salt. In a small bowl, combine egg, yogurt, oil, and vanilla. Stir egg mixture into flour mixture just until all ingredients are moistened. Fold rhubarb and strawberries into batter.

Divide batter between 12 greased muffin cups. Sprinkle tops generously with sugar or glaze with Powdered Sugar Icing after baking. Bake in preheated oven at 400°F for 20 to 25 minutes or until golden brown.

POWDERED SUGAR ICING
½ lb. powdered sugar (about 2 cups)
2 to 3 tablespoons milk or half & half

In a large mixing bowl, combine powdered sugar with water until mixture is desired consistency. Add more water for a thinner consistency and less for a thicker consistency.

Makes approximately 1 cup glaze.

FEATHERBED EGGS

For this recipe, the Halquists use local farm-fresh eggs from free range chickens.

1 slice of country French bread, ¾ inch thick
1 cup of extra-sharp cheddar cheese, grated
¼ cup diced ham (optional)
3 eggs
Half & half
Pepper, freshly ground

Cover bottom of buttered 1-quart casserole dish with one layer of country French bread. Tuck in bread pieces to fill any spaces. Cover with grated sharp cheddar. Sprinkle with diced ham. Mix eggs and half & half to make 1 cup of liquid (approximately ½ cup half & half). Drizzle egg/half & half mixture over top of cheese and ham. Grate pepper over the top. Cover and refrigerate overnight.

Put in cold oven and turn oven to 350°F. Bake, uncovered, for about 45 minutes until puffy and lightly golden.

JIM'S STUFFED FRENCH TOAST

4 cups country French bread, cut into ¾-inch cubes

6 oz. cream cheese, cut into ½-inch cubes

3 eggs

½ cup half & half

⅛ cup real maple syrup

3 tablespoons butter, melted

Layer half of the bread cubes in the bottom of a 1-quart buttered casserole dish. Scatter cream cheese cubes evenly over bread cubes. Cover with remaining bread cubes. Mix eggs, half & half, maple syrup and melted butter. Drizzle over bread/cream cheese mixture.

Preheat oven to 350°F. Bake, uncovered, for 45 to 50 minutes, until top of cubes are golden brown. Serve with berry sauce and maple syrup.

MINNESOTA CHOCOLATE CAKE WITH CREAM CHEESE FROSTING

Makes one 9x13-inch pan or two 9-inch round cake pans

2 cups unbleached flour

1½ cups white sugar

½ cup unsweetened baking cocoa

1 teaspoon salt

1 tablespoon baking soda

1 cup buttermilk

1 cup brewed espresso or strong coffee

⅔ cup canola oil

1 egg

1 teaspoon vanilla extract

Preheat oven to 350°F. In large mixing bowl, stir together flour, sugar, cocoa, salt, and soda. Add buttermilk, coffee, oil, egg, and vanilla. Beat until batter is smooth. (Batter will be thin.) Pour into greased cake pan(s).

Bake for about 30 minutes at 350°F or until cake tests done with a toothpick. Cool before frosting.

CREAM CHEESE FROSTING

12 oz. cream cheese

4 tablespoons soft, sweet cream butter (unsalted)

1 teaspoon vanilla extract

2½ cups powdered sugar

Juice from ½ lemon

In a medium mixing bowl, combine cream cheese, butter, vanilla extract, and powdered sugar; beat until smooth. Beat in lemon juice. Adjust vanilla, lemon juice, and powdered sugar to taste.

Frost cooled cake.

NEW SCENIC CAFÉ

Bay Produce

The menu at the New Scenic Café is affected, in part, by the migratory patterns of Lake Superior's herring, which move from the north shore to the south shore based on weather and seasonal patterns. Their behavior is not well understood by restaurant supply companies, but Scott Graden, New Scenic's chef and co-founder, has a close connection to those who bring him the silver fish. "I get herring from a couple of gentleman who fish out of Knife River, up the road from me — until the herring switch sides. Then I buy from Bodin's out of Bayfield on the south shore," Scott says.

Scott Graden

Fish are important to the New Scenic, but so are a myriad of other local ingredients. Fortunately, Bay Produce's tomatoes aren't migratory. Each time the New Scenic staff heads into Duluth to pick up food from their favorite suppliers, they also cross the bridge and visit Bay Produce in Superior, Wisconsin.

During the twenty years that Bay Produce has been anchored in Superior, they have always delivered the quality insisted upon by Scott for his restaurant. Debbie Gergen, the director of Challenge Center, oversees twenty-five people who grow, prune, harvest, and pack the fruit from Bay Produce's ten thousand tomato plants. "There is a woman with cerebral palsy who works in the packing house," Debbie says. "She is probably the best packer on our staff when it comes to quality standards. If I ever pack with her, she'll slap my hands if I don't pack to the standards she wants."

Nailing down a definition for quality at the New Scenic is challenging. It has a Zen-ness to it, a sense one can taste but not exactly name. It might be captured in the excitement in the Bay Produce staff when they spy the first lemon-colored tomato blossom. Or perhaps it's reflected in the enthusiastic, "Here comes New Scenic, Here comes New Scenic!" that the packing crew occasionally shouts when the café's staff come down to visit Bay Produce's acre and a half of greenhouses.

"The New Scenic has experimented with a number of different tomato dishes," says Debbie, who also oversees shipping of tomatoes to large grocers, wholesalers, and small cafés. "When they were trying some green tomato dishes, we were able to provide them with what they needed. Not only have we been able to supply them with not-just-your-typical tomatoes, we've tried to accommodate their needs for any recipe they might be working on."

There is a pathway between Bay Produce employees carefully selecting — out of thousands — just the right green tomatoes and the quality of food brought to the tables for the delight of New Scenic diners. That's partly because Scott, Debbie, and their respective staffs refuse to accept the industrial model of food production as an end. Rather, fine taste, high levels of customer service, and meaningful work are ends, and the industrial models of efficiency and low cost are tools that can be adapted to meet those ends.

Another signpost on that path is an insistence on integrity. For example, diners and chefs alike enjoy the New Scenic's perennial and annual flower, plant, and herb garden, where fresh and functional herbs, such as tarragon, sage, rosemary, and chives, enhance their cooking and eating experiences. The herb garden was a collective effort of Lissa Ritchie Gardening (of Minnetonka), Scott, and his former business partner, Rita Bergstedt, after the café was purchased in 1999. The foliage transformed the front of the building and made the name "New Scenic" more honest, Scott notes.

"The herb garden is a value that's wrapped around the building," he says. "It greets our customers, like the smile on the server's face. It's a great place to wander; it makes people understand there are real people here getting their hands dirty. No corporation would do that." Picking herbs out the back door, or driving down the cold road in February to get vine-ripened tomatoes, allows Scott to obtain food that springs from the earth and the hands and minds of his neighborhood.

Scott's list of local suppliers is a yard long. He picks up fresh fruit from Sharri Zoff at Sharri's Berries. Louis Jenkins, a local poet, supplies him with mushrooms. Dave Rogotske, of Simple Gifts Syrup and Salmon, lives nearby and provides New Scenic with Alaskan King salmon and halibut. Another neighbor, Katie Hacker, brings in the eggs. Don Mount, of Clover Valley Forest Products, provides syrup. And Al's Dairy, a locally owned father and son operation, delivers Kemps dairy products. Although Kemps is a Minneapolis dairy, Al and his son are right down the road, and Scott likes to keep his money in the community.

Scott's customers and staff know that "right down the road" defines many of New Scenic's suppliers; it is, in part, the basis for their loyalty. So when New Scenic began serving Hawaiian Ahi tuna, some eyebrows were raised. "People have made comments like, 'why are you serving fish from Hawaii' or 'why don't you just have local lake trout?'" Scott notes. "It's an interesting dichotomy of values, because for as much as I want to eat as local as possible, my business strategy also includes offering foods that no one else does. Ahi is obviously not local, but the quality is there."

"Take my smoked duck breast as another example," Scott says. "I get the ducks from a Canadian company but have them processed by Eric Goerdt at Northern Waters Smokehaus in Duluth. We developed a brine and smoking

Scott Graden and Knife River fisherman Stephen Dahl

process, and he's been smoking duck for me every fall for the last four or five years. We worked together on it until we hit it right on the head."

So even the duck and the tuna come from hands connected to hearts, as well as heads, like those at Bay Produce, Al's Dairy, or the herb garden that replaced a parking lot. Out of those joined hands emerges a cuisine unique to the New Scenic Café that Scott calls American. It is American because it is unconfined, like jazz and rap, but also classical, like Copland. It's a culinary tune that, could they hear, would bring the herring back to the North Shore, and to the New Scenic Café, in a flash.

ORGANIC TOMATO AND HERB OIL APPETIZER

This is a great summer appetizer or salad course that couples well with artisan cheese and breads, as well as grilled foods. Enjoy with a crisp white wine, Burgundy Chardonnay, or Pinot Grigio.

2 large organic tomatoes
1 tablespoon cilantro oil
2 teaspoons white truffle oil
¼ cup micro greens
Sea salt and fresh ground pepper mélange to taste

Prepare the cilantro oil (below). Wash the tomatoes and slice into ¼-inch thick slices. Place them spiraling around a large plate or small platter. Drip the cilantro oil and truffle oil randomly over the tomatoes. Sprinkle with sea salt and freshly ground pepper mélange.

CILANTRO OIL

You could substitute almost any herb — such as chives or basil — for a different flavor.

½ lb. cilantro, washed well
½ cup olive oil
½ teaspoon kosher salt

Boil a small pot of water. Place ice and water in a small bowl. Plunge small bunches of cilantro in boiling water for 2 seconds. Remove and immediately plunge into the ice water; let cool.

Remove from the ice water and squeeze the water out. Cut the stems off and chop the leaves. Place in a food processor with the oil and salt and purée for 60 seconds. Place a strainer over a pitcher and scrape the cilantro mix into the strainer.

Let stand for 1 hour. Discard the solids; pour the oil into a small tube. Label, date, and refrigerate.

NORTHERN WATERS SMOKED SALMON APPETIZER

This dish would go nicely with an Alsace Riesling or Gewurztraminer. It can also be modified into a great salad by increasing the greens and tossing all of the ingredients together. Serve the baguette on the side.

Serves 6–8

8-oz. portion smoked salmon
4-oz. wheel of herbed Boursin cheese
1 cup mixed greens
½ Granny Smith apple

Roasted Garlic Vinaigrette (recipe below)
1 baguette

Slice the baguette into ¼-inch-thick pieces and toast in 350°F oven for 10 minutes. Toss the greens with a small amount of garlic vinaigrette. Slice the apple into thin half-moon slices.

Place greens in the center of plate. Place smoked salmon on one side and cheese on the other side. Place sliced apple in the center of greens. Arrange toasted baguette around the plate.

ROASTED GARLIC VINAIGRETTE

This recipe makes almost two cups of vinaigrette. Store in the refrigerator in a covered glass container.

1 cup garlic cloves, peeled and cleaned
½ cup balsamic vinegar
1 cup olive oil
¼ teaspoon cracked black pepper
1 chipotle pepper

Salt to taste

Roast garlic cloves on a sheet pan in a 300°F oven until garlic turns brown and starts to soften, about 30 minutes.

Place garlic, vinegar, black pepper, and the chipotle pepper in a food processor and process until smooth. Slowly add the olive oil, while the machine is running, to emulsify. Add salt as needed.

BITTERSWEET CHOCOLATE GANACHE FONDUE

½ cup heavy cream
½ cup dark bittersweet chocolate chips (about 70% cocoa)
½ cup strawberries
3 kiwi
1 banana
Other seasonal local fruit
½ cup whipped cream
3 oz. Camembert cheese

Bring the cream to a slow boil. Place the chocolate chips in a large dry bowl. Pour the hot cream over the chips. Stir until smooth and keep warm until ready to use.

In mixer, whip heavy cream until stiff peaks form. Add 1 tablespoon sugar, if sweetened cream is desired. Cut the fruit and cheese into 1-inch chunks. Pour the chocolate ganache into a fondue bowl. Place the fondue bowl on a serving plate and surround with the fruit and cheese. Place dollops of whipped cream on fruit. Serve with skewers or fondue forks for dipping.

PINE AND LAKE COUNTRY

PRAIRIE BAY RESTAURANT

The Farm on St. Mathias

"The whole food scene is changing," says Prairie Bay Chef Matt Annand, "and we're trying to be on the forefront up here." "Up here" is Baxter, Minnesota. The forefront is a synthesis of made-from-scratch Minnesota classics influenced by Matt's experience at New York's Culinary Institute, restaurants in Napa Valley and Arizona, and his extensive international travel.

Prairie Bay's tuna noodle hot dish is an example of a Minnesota-classic makeover. It's Asian-inspired with seared Ahi tuna on top of soba noodles. It has a lot of cilantro, fresh ginger, bell peppers, and chilis. "While we try to be fun and inventive, there's nothing crazy or over-intellectualized," Matt says. "I grew up north of here, and I have a pretty good idea what people will eat. I know we're pushing things a little; however, people are becoming more interested in food."

One influence that is changing people's perception of food is the coming-of-age of television cooking shows. "It's kind of ridiculous," Matt says. "You become a chef so you can hide in the kitchen, and then they put chefs on television."

While one aspect of Matt's personality cringes at the thought of televised kitchen melodrama, another delights in

Matt Annand

performance cooking. Prairie Bay features a chef's bar, which allows eight diners to look into the eye of the kitchen's storm and be served specially prepared dishes.

When people come to the chef's bar, Matt asks them if they have any dietary restrictions, food allergies, or foods they dislike. Being sure to avoid those things, he and his cooks then put their talent to work. "It's fun for the customers to watch cooks create on the fly," Matt says. "We always do different things — we'll take menu items and transform them — incorporating whatever is in season.

"It keeps our cooks interested and gets their creative juices flowing," Matt continues. "People want to see the chef, and I like to talk to people. They want to know what's coming up on the menu and what the recipe is. We share those, but we don't actually work with many recipes except when we're baking. We cook by technique, so we'll jot that down along with a basic recipe to follow."

Cooking by technique, cooking from scratch, and performance cooking are part of the recipe that Matt believes will keep Prairie Bay out in the forefront. So will buying the freshest, tastiest, local ingredients. Matt orders daily from his list of local farmers and producers. He'll call Bill Linder for shiitake, wild-crafted mushrooms and duck. He'll call Forest Mushrooms, out of St. Joseph, for his other mushrooms. A woman a few miles up the road gets a call when he needs asparagus in the spring. And he's got Al Jabs' number memorized.

"I sold my dairy cows three years ago," Al says, "and now I'm doing this." "This" is growing heirloom potatoes, tomatoes, melons, broccoli, and a whole palette of vegetables. When Al starts ticking off his potato varieties, it's impossible to keep up. "I have Rose Finn, Purple Viking, Purple Peruvian, a lot of different fingerling varieties. . . ."

Al, who has been growing these venerable potato varieties since he was a kid, is on the leading edge of an agricultural shift in north central Minnesota. He saves enough potatoes for seed each season and plants them back the next. He has as many tomato varieties as potatoes, but he doesn't bother naming each of them. "I've got all colors from white to black," he says. "There are, of course, some red varieties, just like there are some orange carrots among the white and purple varieties."

But Al isn't just a farmer who delights in discovering and growing varieties that have been lost in the nooks and crannies of the Great Horn of Plenty. He has a plan: to open a farm store where he will sell his melons, potatoes, tomatoes and his white carrots. He'll sell other farmers' meats and grind grain into flour with his mill.

Al's wild plan has some credibility because of what he's done so far. He, along with partners Bob and Arlene Jones, started a subscription agriculture project in 2005 with about sixty members — an impressive startup for a community-supported agriculture (CSA) initiative. This year their farm, which they call The Farm, has 120 members.

"I think people like it because we're doing something different," Al says. "The heirlooms are popular out on the East and West Coasts, but they're not widely available here yet. The taste is really incredible."

The taste, variety, and quality of The Farm's products have made Matt Annand at Prairie Bay a loyal customer. He's lucky

Al Jabs

because Al's CSA customers have to come first. Al has had to put some of the area's big resort restaurants on a waiting list. But he calls loyal customers like Matt "business associates."

The Al Jabs–Matt Annand partnership is, as Matt says, nothing crazy. Eaters in north central Minnesota seem prepared for white carrots, orange watermelon, black tomatoes, and the chef's bar as long as they know hot dish is still available. It's a chef-producer fusion that may keep both men in the forefront of the changing food and agriculture scene.

PRAIRIE BAY PIZZA MARGHERITA

FRESH AND EASY PIZZA DOUGH
Yield: 2 14-inch pizza circles

$1/4$-oz. package active dry yeast
1 teaspoon sugar
1 cup warm water
1 tablespoon extra virgin olive oil
$3\frac{1}{2}$ cups all-purpose flour
1 teaspoon kosher salt

In a bowl, combine yeast, sugar, and water and let sit for 8 to 10 minutes; stir in olive oil.

In a food processor, combine flour and salt for 10 seconds. Add the liquid mixture a little at a time while processing, until a ball is formed that isn't sticky. Add a little more flour if necessary.

Remove dough from processor and knead by hand for 3 to 5 minutes. Place in an oiled bowl and cover. Put in a warm place to rise for an hour, or until doubled in size.

Cut in half and roll (or press) each half into $1/4$- to $1/8$-inch thickness, or approximately a 14-inch circle. Place on pizza screen or lightly floured baking stone.

ROASTED GARLIC CLOVES
1 large garlic bulb
1 teaspoon butter
Salt
Stock or water

Preheat oven to 350°F. In a small container or pan using a double-layered "nest" of aluminum foil, place garlic in oven with butter, a little salt, and stock or water. Cover completely and bake for 45 minutes. Uncover and bake for 10 to 15 minutes more. Cut the very top off the bulb and squeeze to remove roasted cloves.

PIZZA SAUCE
Yield: 2 to $2\frac{1}{2}$ cups

2 cloves garlic, crushed
1 medium onion, diced small
2 tablespoons extra virgin olive oil
28-oz. can Italian plum tomatoes or 5 to 6 seasonal/ripe fresh tomatoes
Pinch cayenne
1 tablespoon sugar
Kosher salt to taste
10 to 12 basil stems, whole (leaves reserved)

In a heavy-bottomed saucepan, sweat onions and garlic in olive oil over low to medium heat until onions become translucent and garlic is very fragrant.

Crush tomatoes and drain well. Add to pan with sugar and cayenne. Season with salt. Cook over medium heat for 15 minutes, stirring occasionally. Add basil stems (reserving leaves for pizza topping) and cook another 5 to 10 minutes. Sauce should be broken down. Do not purée. Remove basil stems and adjust seasonings to taste.

PIZZA ASSEMBLY
2 14-inch Fresh and Easy Pizza Dough circles
Pizza Sauce
$1/2$ bulb Roasted Garlic
Sliced tomatoes
1 cup shredded mozzarella cheese
6 to 12 basil leaves
$1/2$ cup grated Parmesan
1 tablespoon extra virgin olive oil
1 teaspoon fresh ground black pepper

Preheat oven to 450°. Spread sauce over pizza, leaving a half-inch border around outside. Sprinkle roasted garlic cloves, sliced tomatoes, and mozzarella uniformly. Bake on the bottom rack for 10 to 15 minutes or until the top and crust are golden brown. Top with basil leaves, olive oil, and fresh ground pepper.

WILD MUSHROOM STRUDEL

This strudel is very versatile — use as an appetizer, a brunch dish, or as a side with any entrée, especially game. Great paired with the Sweet Corn Polenta.

Yield: 8 strudels

Canola or neutral cooking oil (as needed)

4 cups brushed and cleaned medium mushrooms, chopped (whatever is in season)

¼ cup Roasted Garlic Cloves; use the same method as used with Margherita Pizza

1 medium onion, diced small

2 bunches (about 4 to 5 cups) cleaned, stemmed spinach

1 tablespoon water

½ cup chevre (goat cheese)

¾ tablespoon lavender flowers, finely chopped (or fresh thyme or rosemary)

1 cup finely grated Parmesan cheese

1 sprig rosemary, finely chopped

Salt and pepper to taste

16 sheets phyllo dough

½ cup melted butter

White truffle oil, for garnish (optional)

STUFFING

Season each step with just a little salt to enhance flavor.

Preheat a sauté pan over medium to high heat, add a little oil and then the dry mushrooms. Sear dry mushrooms for 3 to 5 minutes. Remove. Add 1 tablespoon oil and carmelize onions over medium heat for 5 minutes. Remove. Lower heat and add spinach along with 1 tablespoon water until spinach is wilted. Remove and drain spinach, pressing any residue liquid out. Combine all cooked ingredients in a bowl with chevre, roasted garlic, lavender, Parmesan, rosemary, salt, and pepper.

ASSEMBLY

Pre-heat oven to 400°F. Working quickly to keep delicate sheets from drying out, brush 1 full sheet of dough with melted butter and place another sheet directly over the top. Brush again. Fold in half and brush again, fold in half one more time and brush again. You should now have 8 layers. Place approximately 1/2 cup of stuffing toward the bottom of the rectangle. Fold ends up close and roll tightly to eliminate air pockets. Brush outside with butter. Repeat with remaining sheets and filling.

Precut into pieces of desired size before baking or keep whole. Bake 6 to 10 minutes or until golden brown outside and hot inside. Garnish with white truffle oil.

PRAIRIE BAY SWEET CORN POLENTA

Makes one 9x11-inch pan

1 cup corn meal
1½ cups chicken stock
1 cup heavy cream
1 cup fresh sweet corn kernels
1 tablespoon kosher salt, check seasoning before baking
1 tablespoon fresh thyme or rosemary, chopped
Herbs, roasted mushrooms, and fresh corn, for garnish

In a heavy-bottomed saucepan, add cream and stock. Slowly bring to a simmer while sprinkling in corn meal. Whisk constantly to prevent sticking. Add 1 cup sweet corn, salt, and chopped thyme or rosemary. Lower heat and stir with a wooden spoon for about 15 minutes until mixture is very thick and is no longer "grainy" when tasting.

Spread onto a lightly greased, rimmed cookie sheet or baking pan to an even depth of up to two inches. Refrigerate for at least one hour. Cut into diamonds or any desired shape.

Fry top-side down in a lightly greased sauté pan until golden brown. Flip to warm through.

Garnish with herbs, roasted mushrooms, and fresh corn.

BREWED AWAKENINGS COFFEEHOUSE

Spica Farm

Things often don't turn out the way people expect. Take Joan Foster of Grand Rapids as an example. She had a good year-round job with Headstart, until Congress cut funding and her summer hours were eliminated. She found herself laid off with time on her hands.

Joan's son was sixteen at the time, and teenagers often have impractical ideas that adults should listen to more carefully. Thankfully, in Joan's case, she did. "My son was encouraging me to open a coffee shop," she recalls. "Then, our local cooperative grocery store offered me free rent if I started a coffee shop in the front of the store. How could I turn that down?"

Thus was born Brewed Awakenings, a name coined from the fertile mind of a teenage friend of Joan's son. Soon, Joan and her son set about serving coffee to the co-op's customers. It went well; co-op sales improved. But then summer was over, Joan's son headed off to the arts magnet high school in Minneapolis, and the Headstart job opened up again.

"I fully intended to go back to my job in the fall," Joan says. But she didn't. Now, more than ten years after that fateful summer, travelers on U.S. Highway 2 into Grand Rapids see a sign promoting Brewed Awakenings vegetarian soups. Joan and her husband have moved the coffee shop, for the second time,

Joan Foster

into their own building with a seating capacity of seventy-seven.

That's how life can be. It takes surprising turns as it unfolds. Laurie and Brad Jones can testify to that. Laurie's a public health nurse for Itasca County; Brad's a forester. But they both share a love of horticulture, so they bought a farm on the Swan River not far from Grand Rapids. "We were just going to raise enough food for ourselves," says Brad.

But nature has a way of providing surplus, and the human mind has a way of responding generously. Nowadays, Brad and Laurie's Spica Farm provides a few custom-processed steers to customers who appreciate grass-fed beef. They also grow durham wheat for people who enjoy grinding their own flour for bread. And they deliver vegetables weekly to Brewed Awakenings, when the seasons allow it.

"Customers at Brewed Awakenings know us through our food," Brad says. "It's a cornerstone business in the community because it connects a lot of people." A connection that, from time to time, gets broadcasted over the airwaves. "We have a community radio station in Grand Rapids," Brad says, "and sometimes I'll hear the announcer say, 'I just saw so-and-so down at the coffee shop.'"

Spica Farm vegetables regularly find their way into Joan's fabulous soups — soups that lure new and old customers to the table at Brewed Awakenings. A fall favorite is Golden Autumn soup made with tomato, apple, and orange juices blended together with squash.

"I got that idea out of the *Sunday's at the Moosewood Cookbook*," Joan explains. The Moosewood cookbooks have been an inspiration to Joan. "I never would have thought those three juices could be combined, but they're delicious together," she says. "I turned the Moosewood recipe, a purée called Autumn Gold, into more of a stew with potatoes and celery and named it Golden Autumn." With that same base she makes Golden Bean soup.

"When I started making soups in the co-op grocery, I never wrote any recipes down," she continues. "I'd just walk around the store to see what looked good. One day I'd have soup with rice and beans, the next I'd have pasta, and then I'd have potatoes with something else. It was fun cooking there. They had a huge spice rack that I'd look at and say, 'O-oh-h, this would be good in soup.'"

Joan has compiled a recipe book with the fifty-five original soup recipes from Brewed Awakenings. The soups don't get served in a regular rotation because she likes to take advantage of local, seasonal, and surplus produce; and she obliges customers who lobby for their favorites. "My tomato coconut curry gets served more often because people who have had it really want to have it again," Joan says. "But with seating for seventy-seven people instead of twenty-two, I can make more than one soup a day. Later in the day, we refrigerate any leftover soup for people to take home. A lot of people have allergies, so I want to make sure I have two or three choices."

And Joan isn't stopping at fifty-five soups. There are others emerging. Spica Farm's CSA (community supported agriculture) subscription has had a noted effect on new recipe development. If, for instance, there is a lot of kale in a week's delivery, Joan may create a kale soup. If the ingredients to a new recipe don't quite work out, she'll alter it a little the next time.

The recipe evolves, just like life. You never know how it's going to turn out.

Laurie and Brad Jones

TOMATO COCONUT CURRY SOUP

This soup is very good without the toppings, but the toppings make for a nice presentation and add even more flavor.

Serves 4–6

1¾ quarts fresh tomatoes; chop ¾ quart and puree 1 quart in the blender
Or use:
28 oz. can tomato sauce
28 oz. can diced tomatoes

1½ cups carrots, sliced thin
¾ to 1 tablespoon yellow curry paste; start with the lesser amount and add to taste, this curry is hot!
1 teaspoon salt, adjust as needed
2 cloves minced garlic
⅛ cup apricot preserves
½ cup unsweetened shredded coconut

In a large saucepan or Dutch oven, add ingredients in the order given. Bring to a simmer, and cook until the carrots are tender. Adjust curry and salt, to taste.

Garnish, if you like, with plain unflavored yogurt and chopped chives.

GERMAN POTATO STEW

4 large potatoes, chopped
1 medium onion, chopped
14.5 oz. can sauerkraut (approximately 2 cups)
½ lb. fresh or frozen green beans, cut into bite-sized pieces
Scant tablespoon dry dill or 3 tablespoons fresh dill
½ teaspoon black pepper, freshly ground
3 tablespoons flour
6 oz. sour cream
6 oz. plain unflavored yogurt

Clean and chop potatoes and place in a large saucepan or Dutch oven. Cover with hot water. Bring to a simmer and cook until the potatoes are tender, about 20 minutes. Add the next 4 ingredients. Add more hot water if needed to cover.

In a separate bowl, mix the flour into the sour cream until smooth. Add the sour cream and yogurt to soup. Heat thoroughly and serve.

POTATO SPINACH SOUP

Serves 6

3 cups potatoes, diced
1 large onion, chopped
¹⁄₂ teaspoon salt
¹⁄₄ teaspoon lemon pepper
1 tablespoon fresh basil, chopped
1¹⁄₂ teaspoons fresh rosemary, chopped, or ¹⁄₂ teaspoon dried
1¹⁄₂ teaspoons fresh thyme, chopped, or ¹⁄₂ teaspoon dried
¹⁄₄ cup fresh parsley, chopped

¹⁄₂ lb. fresh spinach, chopped
2 ounces cream cheese
¹⁄₂ cup grated Parmesan cheese
¹⁄₂ cup grated cheddar cheese

Put 5 cups hot water in a large saucepan. Add the first seven ingredients. Simmer until potatoes are tender, about 20 minutes. Add water if needed. Add the rest of the ingredients. Heat and stir until cheese is melted. Salt and pepper to taste.

COUNTRY BED & BREAKFAST

Steve Anderson Sugarbush

Nestled on thirty-five acres of fields and woods just north of Shafer and a short five-mile drive west of historic Taylors Falls is the Country Bed & Breakfast. Lois Barott and her husband Kenneth (Budd) began the B&B in 1982. After Budd's passing in 1999, daughter Sally moved home to the rural countryside to continue the business with her mother.

Visitors are greeted by a large and gracious 130-year-old red brick farmhouse with a spacious deck, gardens, and walking paths leading into the nearby woods. Upstairs, the three guestrooms — the Lavender Room, the Green Room, and the Old Attic Room — are comfortably furnished.

Lois's family moved to the sixty-acre farm in 1938 when she was ten years old. It was still a working farm then, although only the stone foundation of the barn remained. "We had nowhere to put the cows," Lois says, "so we milked them outside."

Then Lois's father and grandfather acquired an old barn from Center City, which had been the livery stable for the Methodist Church. They took it down piece by piece and rebuilt the barn. "That's the existing barn today," Lois explains. "I've had some restoration done to it these past five years by Al Hawkinson. He's a high school classmate of Sally's who specializes in restoring

Lois and Sally Barott

old barns and buildings. It's been a lot of fun, and the restoration continues."

Sally has been researching the history of the farm since the early 1970s. "Only two families have lived here," she says. "The Lars and Ingre Thorsander family and our family. Lars and Ingre came from Småland, Sweden, in 1869 during the famine."

Sally is a Swedish immigrant historian as well as the B&B's marketing and advertising manager. "My grandparents bought the home from the Thorsander family in 1938 and my parents bought it from my grandparents in 1965," she continues. "I have many wonderful memories growing up here with my five siblings. When my parents turned it into a B&B in 1982, we all had to come home and clean out the attic and closets to make space for the guest rooms."

Country Bed & Breakfast has been in operation for twenty-five years. The concept began in the late 1970s after Lois and Budd took a few trips to Sweden. Lois says, "We modeled our B&B on the European-style B&Bs that share their homes with traveling guests each night. The family lives in the home and the guests 'live' that family's culture."

Lois and Sally love telling family stories around the kitchen breakfast table. They know the rhythm and pacing of each of the stories and together weave them into a complete tapestry. With appreciative and loquacious guests, the conversation flows as easily as the Swedish Egg Kaffe (coffee) at their memorable breakfasts. When Lois is serving her buttermilk pancakes, which are so light they nearly float off the plate, she'll tell about her cousin Steve Anderson, in nearby Center City, who provides the maple syrup.

"Steve has been making maple syrup for nearly fifty years," Lois says, as she passes a golden liquid that adds value to her already valuable pancakes. To get Steve's syrup, Lois and Sally have to go visit him. That's what many people in the area do, including WCCO radio and a national television show.

Steve will tell you that he has 1,200 taps. "Sometimes you've got to have that many," he says. "You put three pails on a tree and only one of them may run. I think I should have a stethoscope when I go out there and tap them."

Steve laughs gently when he says stethoscope. He wants to be clear to city-folk this is a joke. There are other mysteries in the sugar bush. In his half century of collecting sap, Steve has experienced a lot of them. One thing he's learned is that he can't predict whether it will be a good year or not.

"I'll give you your forecast on the 15th of April," he says. "It'll be all over with. It isn't any different than putting in 1,000 acres of corn. Is it going to be a good crop or a poor crop? You'll know in October, but not May."

Steve has a particular disdain for prognosticators who make the early season predictions. "I know one year Harold and I were tapping. It was 1977," he says, checking his book of records, which he's kept since the 1960s. "1976 was really a dry summer. On the radio they were saying, those trees are going to die. You can't tap them. We started believing those radio people. We almost thought they knew what they were talking about. It's like anything else on the radio. You don't know if it's true or not."

It wasn't true.

That year when Steve and Harold tapped the trees and started cooking, they worked steady for a month. "Those trees, it didn't matter what the weather did," Steve recalls. "The ground was so dry they said the trees were going to die, you know. It got cool at night. It got warm in the day. The sun shone. It was raining. It didn't make a nickel's worth of difference. Those trees were nuts. We couldn't catch up. It was unbelievable."

After all that, after the best season in half a century, those trees produced sap the next season, too. Some of them are still making sap thirty years later. Steve doesn't know which are stranger: the radio prognosticators making endless predictions, right or wrong, or the trees and their cycles.

He does know that being in the sugar bush for the sap run is a fine thing. He's seventy years old, and he'll likely continue the annual harvest as long as he can. "It's a good place to be in the spring," he says. "Everything is coming to life. You've been boarded up in the house. Then you go out there and the birds are singing and the sun is nice."

But Steve's syrup-cooking partner, Harold Vitalis, passed away five years ago. Something is absent from the brightness of spring that Steve so enjoys, now. He'd made syrup with Harold for more than forty springs and had known Harold since he was five years old.

"We prided ourselves in making fancy syrup instead of making it look dark," Steve says. "I miss my partner."

It's this amber pride of Steve and Harold's sugar bush that Lois and Sally Barott take pleasure in pouring over their morning buttermilk pancakes at the Country Bed & Breakfast.

Steve Anderson

BUDD'S COUNTRY BED & BREAKFAST OMELET

The brown eggs are from Karl and Kris Ruser, Center City; the cucumbers are from the farmer's market in Lindstrom; and the herbs and vegetables are from Sally Barott's herb garden, all organic. The cheese is from Eichten's in Center City.

4 tablespoons margarine

2 tablespoons chopped onion

2 tablespoons chopped green pepper

2 tablespoons chopped fresh mushrooms

3 farm-fresh eggs

1 tablespoon cold water

1 oz. Gouda cheese, grated

1 oz. mild cheddar cheese, grated

Salt and pepper to taste

Heat an omelet pan on high. Add 4 tablespoons of margarine and melt (use margarine, it handles the higher temperature, butter will burn). Add the chopped vegetables and sauté over medium heat until tender, about 3 minutes. In a small bowl, beat the eggs with a fork for 30 seconds. Add the water and continue to beat for another 15 seconds. Add the eggs to the sautéed vegetables. As they cook, pull the eggs away from the sides of the pan. Continue until the omelet is firm enough to flip. Flip with a large spatula and heat the other side of the omelet. Sprinkle the grated cheeses onto the omelet. Fold over the other half to melt the cheese. Salt and pepper to taste.

Garnish with a fresh tomato slice, fresh cucumber slice, chopped chives, and a parsley sprig. Serve immediately.

LOIS'S BUTTERMILK PANCAKES

The maple syrup is from Steve Anderson, Lois's cousin in Center City.

2½ cups unbleached flour

2½ tablespoons baking powder

¼ cup granulated sugar

1 teaspoon salt

3 farm-fresh eggs

2 cups buttermilk (shake the carton well before measuring)

2 teaspoons vanilla

In a large bowl, mix the dry ingredients together. Add the eggs, buttermilk, and vanilla. Mix with on medium speed until the batter is smooth, about 2 minutes. Using a ¼ cup, pour pancakes onto a preheated cast iron griddle that has been oiled with shortening. A non-stick griddle will also work. Flip the pancakes over when the top starts to bubble. Heat the other side until golden brown.

Serve with fresh country butter and homemade maple syrup.

RED RIVER VALLEY

CARIBOU GRILL

Double J Elk

Build it and they will come. Nobody takes that little phrase seriously. Nobody, that is, except some people in Hallock, population 1,200, in far northwestern Minnesota.

"Since we opened in January 2004, it's been busy a lot for lunches, on the weekend, and in the evening when there is an event in town," says Kristen Blomquist, one of the co-owners of Hallock's Caribou Grill. "I think people come because the food is good. They drive over from North Dakota, and we also have friends who come from forty-five miles away."

Friends and neighbors are far apart in Kittson County, where Hallock is the county seat, so forty-five miles may not be a vast distance. But the Caribou Grill offers rewards not available in other small-town restaurants and cafes. Rewards such as grilled, baked, or blackened salmon fillets; a porterhouse pork chop; a pork tenderloin covered in cream sauce with mushrooms and peppers; or scaloppine with rainbow fettuccini topped with artichoke hearts and mushrooms in a rich, creamy sauce.

"Our cook, Dawn Lindstrom, is great," Kristen says. "She's more of a home-cooking kind of a cook, not a trained chef. We've tried trained chefs and they tended to have an attitude." One of the issues that those trained chefs had an attitude about was using local ingredients. Their training, Kristen says, led them to prefer standardized units of commoditized food off the back of a corporate food service truck.

Serving up elk steaks at Caribou Grill

But that's not the preferred culinary methodology up north at the Caribou Grill.

"In the summer, Dean, our gardener, will bring in produce for Dawn to use," Kristen explains. "In our first year, our manager and our cooks were not into it. They wanted to predict what they were going to get. But Dean might come in with 10 pounds of green beans, or the green beans he thought would be ripe weren't, so he'll bring in something else. With this system, we know the quality is better than what comes off the truck, but we have to adjust our menu to what's available."

But when Dean's green beans, zucchini, or tomatoes are ripe, they will end up in one of Dawn's homemade soups. She makes two or three soups a day and is famous for them. "My favorite is her tomato," says Kristen. "It's got really chunky bits of tomato in it. Some of the others are clam chowder, pea soup, potato soup, chicken dumpling — she makes her own dumplings — and chicken and rice."

Another occasional rewards that locals and long-distance travelers can enjoy are elk burgers, chili, and steaks.

"Dawn has a secret recipe for making the elk burgers at the Caribou Grill," says Jerod Hanson, whose family raises elk in rural Hallock. Jerod got into elk farming in 1999 as a way to earn some extra income. Although bull-antler velvet and breeding stock have been the mainstays of the small United States elk industry, Jerod chose to focus on sales of meat. In addition to selling ground meat, he sells steaks like ribeye, New York strip, and sirloin. Elk dishes are not regularly on the menu at the Caribou Grill because Jerod cannot keep up with the demand. The fact that they are there at all puts the restaurant on equal footing with some pretty upscale urban eateries.

Elk meat is known for its great taste, but in the U.S. it is rare. When it is available, it is often imported frozen from New Zealand. For many years, domestic elk were so valuable as breeding stock that they were rarely sold for their meat. However, times have changed and elk meat is currently competitive with all natural or organically grown beef and has the benefit of being lower in fat and cholesterol.

That's good for diners at the Caribou Grill. It's also fine with Jerod because it creates a niche for his farm's product. He likes raising elk because they don't require as much labor as beef cattle. In addition to their low maintenance requirements, they also use pasture more efficiently. But Jerod, like all livestock farmers in northwestern Minnesota, suffers from a lack of processing facilities. When he's ready to convert living elk into ribeye and chili, he has to take the animal almost 150 miles to a small plant in Barnesville.

It's possible the region could support another small meat-processing plant. After all, Kristen and her business partners built a fine-dining restaurant on the northern prairie and the diners did come. They came as individuals and in groups, for employee Christmas parties and political party meetings, for a drink at the bar and to listen to Miss North Dakota sing in the lounge. And while making the business work financially hasn't been easy, Kristen and her partners have built a community resource appreciated by people for miles around.

STRAWBERRY SPINACH SALAD

Serves 8

16 cups fresh spinach, washed and torn into bite-sized pieces
4 cups fresh strawberries, sliced
½ cup fresh bacon, fried, drained, and in small pieces
½ cup slivered almonds, toasted
½ cup Parmesan cheese, shredded
4 eggs, hard-boiled and cut in chunks

Combine all ingredients and serve with a raspberry vinaigrette dressing.

Bluefin Bay of Tofte, Minnesota, makes a good raspberry vinaigrette, which is readily available. You can also add bite-sized pieces of roasted chicken to this salad.

BARBECUE BACON ELK BURGER

This is so unexpectedly delicious in its simplicity.
1 serving

⅓ lb. ground elk, formed into a patty
Salt and pepper to taste
1 slice cheddar cheese
2 slices onion, fried
2 slices smoky bacon, fried
1 tablespoon of your favorite BBQ sauce
1 multi-grain bun, buttered and toasted
Lettuce, tomato, and pickles to garnish

Separately fry the onions and bacon to desired doneness. Sprinkle salt and pepper on both sides of the burger and rub it in. Grill the elk burger, and toast the bun while the meat is being grilled. Elk is low-fat, so try not to overcook for best flavor. Add the cheese to the hot burger about a minute after turning; cook another couple of minutes and remove from the heat.

Put the burger on the bun, add bacon, sauce, onion, and other garnish, and enjoy.

CORN CHOWDER

Serves 8–10

1 small onion
2 ribs celery, diced
¼ cup red pepper, diced
¼ cup green pepper, diced
1 clove garlic, minced
2 russet potatoes, diced
2 cups fresh shucked corn (frozen will work in the off season)
1 quart chicken stock
1 quart milk
½ cup butter

½ cup flour
Salt, pepper, and chopped fresh parsley to taste

Melt the butter and sauté all vegetables, except the corn and potatoes, until the onions are translucent. Sprinkle flour over the vegetables and continue cooking for one minute, stirring constantly. Slowly add the stock and milk, stirring constantly. Add corn, potatoes, and seasonings. Simmer for 20 minutes, stirring often. Salt and pepper to taste, garnish with chopped parsley.

LOGHOUSE & HOMESTEAD ON SPIRIT LAKE

Jake's Syrup and Natural Products

It wasn't until her mother broke her ankle that Suzanne Tweten really learned to cook. "My mother is a superb cook, but she'll admit that she is a terrible teacher," Suzanne says. "She's one of those people who sets out to teach you and ends up saying, 'here, let me show you.' When I started running the bed and breakfast, I knew how to cook two things — béarnaise and krumkake — but I had no clue about basics, like how to sift flour."

Suzanne's culinary journey began when she decided to help out her parents at their bed and breakfast near Vergas, Minnesota. Lyle and Yvonne Tweten had converted the family's 1902 three-story farmhouse and 1889 log house into the Loghouse and Homestead Bed and Breakfast in the early 1990s.

One of Suzanne's first tasks was converting her mother's mental recipe file into written form. She succeeded in translating Yvonne's "a pinch of that and a bit of this" to tablespoons and teaspoons, but she was still only a paper chef. "It took me a year to make banana bread," Suzanne recalls. "I had absolutely

Suzanne Tweten

no confidence. Then my mother broke her ankle, and she had to stay off her feet."

Guests coming from across the United States and, from time to time, the globe were not going to wait until Yvonne's ankle healed to get their breakfast. Suzanne was going to have to sink or swim as the Loghouse and Homestead's new chief of culinary services. So she flapped her wings tentatively, became airborne, and has soared ever since.

"My mother insists I have the talent passed down from my French great-grandmother," Suzanne says. Her French toast would likely intrigue and make her great-grandmother proud. She uses challah, a Jewish holiday bread, and fills it with a cream cheese and maple syrup combination. The French toast is served in the sitting room of the guest's bedroom, with fresh-squeezed orange juice, a fruit coulis, and, if the guest eats meat, a smoked pork and wild rice sausage patty.

Beside the smoked pork and wild rice sausage, the Loghouse serves a potato sausage, obtained from a butcher in Detroit Lakes, and a smoked country sausage, purchased from

Goodman's grocery in Vergas. The sausages link Suzanne to her local hamlet, but it's the maple syrup that truly binds her to the land and the community.

The sugar bush on Suzanne's land yields sap for neighbor Jerry Jacobsen, of Jake's Syrup, to cook into the maple delight that Suzanne serves to her customers. Recently, Suzanne developed a forest stewardship plan that will nurture more maple trees on her 115-acre farm. Along with the maple, basswood — maple's constant companion tree in Minnesota — will be encouraged.

The Twetens' interest in local forests is nothing new. In the late 1990s, Suzanne's parents started the annual Maplefest in Vergas. On the first Saturday in April, people come to visit the area's sugar houses, partake in a feast at the community center, and share in the celebration of the spring ritual of gathering sweet sap.

On a brisk spring morning when the sun is beginning to rise over Spirit Lake — which is just outside the door of the farmhouse — and the sap is once again rising in the maples, guests can gaze out over the lake and woods from the third-story Fredhom room. From this view, one can visually cross the lake to the tall oak, embracing a vast eagle's nest, and contemplate the rising and setting of the sun and the turning of the seasons. It is good to wake up that way.

Then there will be a gentle rap on the door. On opening it, guests will find a cart with a carafe of hot coffee — Muskrat Coffee from nearby Native Harvest — hot water for tea and perhaps some of the delicious banana bread Suzanne worked so hard to learn to bake. Also, if you wish to be distracted from your contemplation, you can read the *Fargo Forum* that Suzanne has left for you.

This she calls "pre-breakfast."

Later, as you sit down for your full breakfast, Suzanne will say hopefully, "When I went to town to get the newspaper, it looked like the ice was just getting ready to go out on some of the lakes."

It will be one more sign of the coming season. Soon afterward the perennial herbs will rouse themselves in Suzanne's garden. A garden with annuals — tomatoes, corn, and zucchini — will follow them. Then — and this is hard to think of in April — the wild plums, chokecherries, and gooseberries ripen and Suzanne will make jellies to serve to her guests.

It is this engagement, and then release, of the seasons that keeps Suzanne in love with the land her family has been a part of for so long. It is this natural elegance she wishes to share with her guests.

WILD RICE SAUSAGE

Makes 8 patties

1¾ cups chicken broth
1 cup Native Harvest wild rice
1 bay leaf
½ cup chopped onions

1 teaspoon fresh thyme, chopped
¾ teaspoon fresh rosemary, chopped

Simmer all ingredients for 25 minutes. Mix with one pound (or more) of your favorite local sausage. Form into patties and sauté until cooked through.

MAPLE PECAN FRENCH TOAST

This is so easy and so good.

1 loaf of challah bread
8 eggs
¾ cup half & half
¼ cup sugar
1 teaspoon vanilla
Pinch of salt

FILLING

8 ounces cream cheese, softened
¼ teaspoon vanilla
2 tablespoons fresh-squeezed orange juice

¼ cup pure maple syrup
1½ cups pecans, coarsely chopped

Soak 8 (¾-inch thick) slices of challah bread in the egg and half & half mixture. A large cake pan or jelly roll pan works well. Let set for 15 minutes, turn occasionally to saturate all areas of the bread.

Butter a 9x13-inch cake pan. Sprinkle half of the pecans on the bottom. Lay 4 slices of the saturated bread on the pecans. Spread the filling on top of the bread. Top with the 4 remaining slices of bread. Layer with the remaining pecans.

Bake at 350ºF for 30 minutes. Serve with fresh hot maple syrup.

SPOON BREAD IN A MUG

Soak ¾ cup stone-ground cornmeal in 1 cup of cold water. Set aside.

Brown and break up ½ to ¾ pound of your favorite local breakfast sausage (half hot and half regular gives a great flavor). You could also add 1 to 2 green onions, chopped, for additional flavor.

Beat together the following ingredients and let sit while browning the meat:
2 tablespoons minced green onion, white and green
1 cup buttermilk
3 eggs, beaten
⅓ cup grated Parmesan cheese

¾ teaspoon salt
1 tablespoon sugar

Put 1 cup hot water in a saucepan and bring to a boil. Quickly add cornmeal mixture, whisking continuously. Cook 2 minutes until thick.

Remove from stove and add the cooked sausage and buttermilk/egg mixture. Blend well. Spoon into greased mugs. Fill about three quarters full. Sprinkle with Parmesan cheese.

Place mugs (or ramekins) on a cookie sheet or cake tin for easy handling. Bake at 375°F for about 30 to 35 minutes, until puffy and slightly browned. Serve the spoonbread with glazed apple slices.

GLAZED APPLE SLICES

Melt ¼ cup white sugar in a non-stick pan over moderately high heat. Add two apples, each cut into eight wedges. Stir quickly while coating with the glaze; don't overcook.

Garnish each mug with a sprig of fresh herbs and place the ramekin or mug on a plate with apple wedges alongside.

Cook's Note: If you don't have oven-proof mugs, use ramekins. Four-ounce ramekins will provide about 10 servings; decrease your cooking time by 5 minutes.

SPIRITED BAKED APPLES

Serves 4

Core 4 slightly tart local apples like Harralsons and remove a strip around each to reduce the chance of bursting while baking. Place in a 9-inch square glass baking dish.

Fill the cored hole in each apple with brown sugar and press down to pack. Add a teaspoon of butter, press down. Add a few currants and nuts. Add a little brown sugar and sprinkle with Watkins Apple Bake spice, or a mixture of cinnamon and allspice.

Add $\frac{1}{3}$ cup brown sugar and 3 tablespoons of butter, broken into pieces, into the baking dish. Pour in $\frac{1}{3}$ cup each of water and bourbon (or brandy).

Bake in a 375°F preheated oven for 1 hour. Apples should be soft when pierced with a toothpick. Baste every 15 minutes. If apples show signs of bursting before they are soft, pierce with the point of a sharp knife. Serve warm.

Suzanne serves the apples in pretty footed dishes and spoons the sauce over each apple. Serve with heavy cream.

PUFF PANCAKE WITH STRAWBERRY-ALMOND BUTTER

Incredibly delicious and impressive brunch dish. Serves 2

In small bowl of mixer, beat 3 eggs and $\frac{1}{4}$ teaspoon almond extract until foamy.

Beat in alternately at low speed, $\frac{3}{4}$ cup milk and $\frac{3}{4}$ cup sifted flour until very smooth.

Melt $\frac{1}{4}$ cup butter in a 12" ovenproof skillet. Pour in batter and bake at 425°F for 20 to 25 minutes.

Cut in half and place on two plates. Serve with strawberry-almond butter and fresh strawberries. Suzanne does this with raspberries when they are in season.

STRAWBERRY-ALMOND BUTTER

In a food processor, cream together one stick of butter ($\frac{1}{2}$ cup) with 2 cups of powdered sugar. Add $\frac{1}{2}$ cup of toasted sliced almonds and $1\frac{1}{2}$ cups fresh, washed, and hulled strawberries. Pulse until blended.

Serve butter mixture and additional fresh berries in pretty footed bowls.

MINWANJIGE CAFE

Native Harvest

"Turn right at Richwood and go seven or eight miles and you'll see us right across from the Strawberry Lake store," Janice Chilton will tell a caller asking for directions to the Minwanjige Cafe. Strangers may not know how to locate this small cafe on the White Earth Reservation in Becker County, but ever since it opened in 2005, the widespread White Earth community, tourists, and summer cottage dwellers know how to find their way.

That's partly because the cafe serves great food and the staff are attentive to customer needs. Before taking your order, they will ask if you are a vegetarian. If you are, they will return shortly — very shortly — with the sandwich and soup of the day for their vegetarian clientele. "We like our customers to be happy," Janice says.

Chances are, the soup will include wild rice as a base. That's because Minwanjige Cafe is a project of the White Earth Land Recovery Project, whose stated mission is to "facilitate recovery of the original land base of the White Earth Indian Reservation, while preserving and restoring traditional practices of sound land stewardship, language fluency, community development and strengthening our spiritual and cultural heritage."

Fortunately for everybody who visits the cafe, good food in the form of wild rice, maple syrup, hominy corn, and buffalo, along with strawberries, cranberries, raspberries, and plums, is central to the path toward land, cultural, and spiritual recovery.

Wild Rice Soup

Organically grown, fair trade Muskrat coffee, although not a traditional food for the Anishinaabe people of White Earth, is also served at Minwanjige Cafe.

"I never liked a cup of coffee where you could still see the cup's bottom when it was full," Janice says. The bold Muskrat coffee is roasted by Winona LaDuke, founder of the White Earth Land Recovery Project and former Green Party vice-presidential candidate.

Winona's vision for land recovery at White Earth is also bold because the White Earth Band of Chippewa, or Anishinaabe as they prefer to be called, were granted 837,000 acres (1,300 square miles) of magnificent land in northwestern Minnesota by a treaty signed by the United States Senate on March 19, 1867. By the 1930s, just over half a century after the Senate signed the binding treaty, ninety-five percent of the reservation had been taken from the Anishinaabe and transferred into non-Indian hands. With the loss of their land, the culture of the Anishinaabe came crashing down upon the people.

"Our land sustains our spirit," Winona says. "The loss of our land has meant the loss of our traditional values." With the land went the language. Along with that also went the traditional foods, but they are now returning as part of the fare available at Minwanjige Cafe.

Important traditions surrounding certain foods mean that the Minwanjige Cafe sometimes moves outdoors. In early

April, the cafe celebrates the collecting of the first maple syrup with a feast in the sugar bush. At the feast there will be swamp tea and buffalo. There will also be wild rice cake. For the cake they use mizon, broken rice grains that have been made into flour. They also use cooked rice, along with locally produced eggs, honey, and maple syrup. Then, just for something really special, they drizzle maple butter over the cake.

The sap, which is collected and boiled during and after the time of the feast, will be bottled and sold via Native Harvest, the retail branch of the White Earth Land Recovery Project. Through Native Harvest's website, mail-order catalog, and various wholesale outlets, customers can buy the fruits of a recovering culture, such as maple syrup, wild rice, raspberry jam, buffalo sausage, wild plum jam, and various crafts created by people in the community.

"Native Harvest's sales have been growing," says Todd Sisson, a food scientist who has been hired to help expand the food processing part of the business. While packaging and processing had been done on site at the restaurant, this part of the business has recently moved to a new, larger facility nearby.

"Minwanjige Cafe is not just a restaurant for the far-flung residents of White Earth," says Todd. "It is a community and commercial center. There is a grand diversity of crafts on display and for sale there." Bev St. John has her elegant ribbon dresses exhibited. Clyde Este brings in his masterful black ash baskets. And Earl and Kathy Houghland have their expertly crafted birch-bark creations displayed. Calvin Moose's bone carvings are also there, along with a beautiful array of quilts and bead and quillwork.

"In the winter, people come here and teach each other the crafts," Todd says. "They can also buy their crafting supplies or take language classes."

Janice is proud of the artisans' work. She says, "A woman who is a potter is going to make a set of dishes for the cafe. People will be able to eat from dishes made especially for us."

There is always a new idea in the works at Native Harvest and Minwanjige Cafe. Janice and her husband Jerry are planning on raising heritage turkeys, such as the Bourbon Red and Bronze breeds, and including their meat in the menu. She is also exploring using grass-fed beef from her family's Scottish Highlander cattle.

All of these items make Minwanjige Cafe a place with a strong vision. Fortunately for diners, it has a nice view, too. The large picture window provides an intimate prospect of a wetland. "People like to order a cup of coffee and just watch the ducks," Janice says. "If we can, we want to put a steel moose sculpture out there."

If you want to find out if the moose made it into the cafe's wetland, give Janice a call. She'll give you directions, too.

"Will you be coming up Highway 10? OK. Take a right at the first stoplights in Detroit Lakes. Follow that road through town seven or eight miles to Richwood. Take a right there. It's pretty easy. Just two rights."

CORN POSOLE BISON STEW

2½ lbs. bison meat, cubed

12 oz. dried blue corn posole

1 medium Spanish onion, chopped

3 cloves garlic, minced

4 fresh jalapeño chilies, seeded and thinly sliced

28 oz. can seasoned diced tomatoes

3 tablespoons sun-dried tomato paste

1(12 oz.) bottle of light beer

3 teaspoons dried cilantro

1 teaspoon dried oregano

1 teaspoon cayenne

Juice of one fresh lime

Tabasco or other hot sauce (optional)

½ teaspoon salt

1½ tablespoons olive oil

Rinse the blue corn posole and soak for 24 hours in enough water to cover. After soaking, rinse and place in a large casserole with enough water to completely cover the posole. Add salt and cook over medium heat for two hours. Turn off the heat and let posole remain in the water until ready for use.

Heat the olive oil over high heat in a Dutch oven. When the oil is hot, add the onion and minced garlic (stir to keep the garlic from burning.) Cook until transparent. Add the meat and lightly brown. Remove any liquid. Add the sliced jalapeños and mix well. Add the tomatoes (liquid included). Drain the blue corn posole thoroughly and add it to the meat. Add the tomato paste, 5 oz. (½ bottle) of beer, and the cilantro, oregano, cayenne, and salt. Cover the casserole and cook on medium heat until the meat is tender. This could take 1 to 3 hours depending on the cut of meat you use. During the cooking process, add the rest of the beer and the lime juice. When the meat seems tender, readjust spices and add salt or Tabasco to taste.

OATMEAL MOLASSES BREAD

Makes 2 loaves, 9x5-inch pans

3 tablespoons yeast

1½ cups molasses

5 cups warm water

4 cups flour

1 cup oatmeal

3 tablespoons butter

1 tablespoon maple syrup

1 teaspoon salt

Combine yeast, molasses, and warm water to proof (place in warm area until bubbles appear). Mix flour, oatmeal, butter, syrup, and salt together. Add to yeast mixture. Work into a smooth dough and knead for 5 minutes. Let rise until doubled. Punch down and divide into two loaves. Let rest for 15 minutes.

Shape loaves into greased pans. Let rise again until doubled in size. Score the tops and drizzle with honey and sprinkle with oatmeal. Bake at 325°F for about 40 minutes.

MINNESOTA RIVER VALLEY

THE AMBOY COTTAGE CAFE

Whole Grain Milling Company

When Lisa Durkee opened the Amboy Cottage Cafe in 2000, it was a testament to her belief that big things can be done in small places. The cafe is a 750-square-foot renovated Pure Oil gas station, which was built in the 1920s with an English Cottage motif. It seats thirty-one people, if you count the bathroom. Seating does expand in the summer when the gazebo and the outdoor picnic tables are brought out. Nevertheless, reservations are a necessity on weekends.

There are other measures of smallness associated with the cafe. Amboy residents number less than the square footage of their cafe — and it is theirs, Lisa will insist. For the conventional economist, the fact that a cafe in a town of about 600 people is regularly packed at lunchtime is big. That the cafe employs about twenty people part-time in such a tiny town is also big. But there's more to that part of the equation than meets the eye.

"I used to be a nurse in Mankato, a forty-minute commute," Lisa explains. "But I wanted a job close to home. It just made more sense economically and ecologically." Lisa has created a non-commuting job for both herself and other community members.

Lisa Durkee

"A lot of people who work here are related," Lisa says. "We have a number of mother-and-daughter and mother-and-son employee combinations." The cafe also has customer-worker ties. "The daughter of the antique dealer across the street works here," Lisa comments. "Her family walks over and eats here two or three times a day."

Relationship webs like that make economic measurement interesting. It turns out that some of the tables and chairs in the cafe belong to the antique shop and are sold and replaced regularly. "They become more antique-y while they are here," Lisa jokes. "We add value to them."

An antique is a small thing an economist probably can quantify. And economists actually coined the term "value-added." Lisa and her staff often talk about another value-added commodity, what they refer to as the cafe community — the people who bring fresh flowers and garden vegetables to the cafe in the summer and contribute to the paperback book exchange. They also provide the art (for sale!) that hangs on the walls.

How do you measure community? Is it big or small? For one thing, it can fix faucets. "I've got a group of men who come in every morning, and sometimes I barter with them," Lisa says. "I ask them if they'll trade a waffle breakfast in exchange for fixing the faucet." Imagine that the cafe community is part of the "big" side of Lisa's "big things in small places" equation — even if it is a small community.

Is the food "big?" Lisa says it's "slow food" — in contrast to the hectic clip of convenience fare. Those customers who have paced their lives to the beat of drive-by meals may consider the cafe's service to be slow — but it's just a subtle form of encouragement for them to relax and enjoy their meal. "We actually take the time to make a pot roast, and my mom still makes all the pie crusts," Lisa says. "I think the people come for the good food."

When the staff takes the time and patience to make that good food, like the slow-cooked pot roast, hand-rolled focaccia bread topped with olive oil, herbs, and mozzarella, or a hand-rolled pizza crust, they hope the diner will also take the time to enjoy it.

Whenever possible, the Amboy Cottage Cafe uses suppliers who share their notion of good service and "slow food." For example, they serve products from Whole Grain Milling of Welcome, Minnesota. The Hilgendorf family, who own the company, grow organic corn on their farm, which they make into delicious corn chips. The corn chips are favorites with the cafe's homemade chili.

The cafe also serves milk, ice cream, and butter from MOMs, which stands for Minnesota Organic Milk. The vanilla, chocolate, and molasses chip ice cream taste homemade and come from nearby Gibbon. Mike, Diane, and Roger Hartman started MOMs in the 1990s as the first on-farm organic dairy creamery in Minnesota. They felt that small creameries could revitalize the countryside, much like the Amboy Cottage Cafe has helped bring a renaissance to Amboy.

"Small, on-farm creameries can make small dairies like ours profitable," says Mike. "That can create economic opportunities in our small towns, and urban people will be drawn back to the rural areas." Since the Hartmans started their creamery a decade ago, a few more dairies have turned to on-farm bottling and processing, but demand continues to grow faster than the supply. "I wish we could get more MOMs' butter," Lisa says. "People just don't understand how good organic milk and dairy products are."

The crew at the Whole Grain Milling Company

The butter shortage reveals the Hartmans' rejection of the corporate model of "expand or die." MOMs' size meets their needs for income and that's good enough. Lisa accepts that idea implicitly.

Lisa and the Hartmans also agree that there is probably a "right" size for MOMs and the Amboy Cottage Cafe — somewhere in the continuum of small. That way the energy created by their economic activity becomes available, at no cost, to others. That is evident in Amboy, where an art gallery has opened up right next door. "I don't think they would have opened if we hadn't been here," Lisa says. "The cafe brings a lot of people in. I only wish we could get a grocery store now."

Perhaps in time that will happen, but for now Lisa is having fun doing her big thing in her small place. She has no intention of returning to her forty-minute commute and her nursing career. "I think I'm doing more here to contribute to people's health than I was working as a nurse in the modern health care system," she says.

NORTHERN LIGHTS SWISS CHARD QUICHE

Serve hot with baked potato and sour cream, or chilled with a tossed salad. Very pretty!

1 medium onion, coarsely chopped
3 tablespoons butter
1½ cups sliced mushrooms
2 cloves garlic, chopped
1 lb. Swiss chard, cleaned and chopped
4 eggs
1 cup cream
1 cup milk
½ teaspoon salt
¼ teaspoon freshly grated nutmeg, plus more for topping
1 cup grated mild white cheese
1 unbaked pie crust
4 slices Swiss cheese

In a large saucepan, sauté onion in butter for a few minutes. Toss in mushrooms and sauté with onions until soft and beginning to brown. Stir in garlic. Immediately add Swiss chard and steam under a cover for a few minutes until the chard is wilted. Remove from heat.

In a separate bowl, mix eggs, cream, milk, salt, nutmeg, and white cheese. Combine cooked vegetables and egg mixture and pour into unbaked piecrust. Top with 4 slices of Swiss cheese and more grated nutmeg. Bake at 350° until browned and interior temperature has reached 160°.

BUTTERNUT BASIL SOUP

Garnish this aromatic soup with paper-thin red apple slices and freshly snipped purple basil leaves.
Breathe deeply!

1 large butternut squash
1 large onion, finely chopped
2 tablespoons butter
2 tablespoons olive oil
3 cloves garlic, chopped
4 teaspoons dried basil
1 quart well-seasoned vegetable or chicken stock
4 slices American or soft cheese
1 teaspoon balsamic vinegar
Brown sugar, to taste
Salt and pepper, to taste

Scrub the butternut squash and microwave for 3 minutes to soften for cutting. Place on a cutting board and cut in half. Do not remove seeds.

Place the halves, cut side down, on a buttered baking sheet. Bake in a 350° oven until soft. Meanwhile, sauté onion with butter and olive oil in your favorite soup pot until translucent. Add garlic and dried basil. Stir for one minute and enjoy a deep whiff!

Quickly add vegetable or chicken stock and let simmer. When the squash is done, remove seeds and process or mash the pulp until it is smooth, adding a bit of the broth if necessary. Combine the purée with the broth and add sliced cheese. If the soup is too thick because the squash was dry, adjust the texture of the soup by adding more broth. Stir in balsamic vinegar.

Taste the soup and add up to 2 teaspoons of brown sugar to enhance the flavor of the squash. Add salt and pepper to taste.

SEEDED OAT AND POTATO BREAD

Perfect with organic butter fresh out of the oven or toasted for the next day's breakfast!

2 tablespoons yeast

2 cups warm water

1 cup milk

½ cup mashed potato

¼ cup brown sugar or 3 tablespoons honey

1 cup regular rolled oats

3 cups whole wheat flour

¼ cup butter, melted

2 tablespoons sea salt

Bread flour, for kneading

3 tablespoons sesame seeds

2 tablespoons flaxseed

⅓ cup sunflower seeds

Additional melted butter for topping

Soften yeast in warm water and milk. Add mashed potato and brown sugar or honey. Stir in rolled oats and 2 cups whole wheat flour. Let the sponge sit for a few minutes while you melt the ¼ cup butter and gather together your sea salt and bread flour. Turn on the radio to some good music or convince a family member to produce some live rhythms for your kneading accompaniment. Add the melted butter and sea salt. Stir well and add 1 more cup of wheat flour, then switch to adding bread flour until the dough becomes stiff enough to knead. Knead until the dough is smooth and elastic.

Oil a bowl to keep the dough from sticking and rotate the ball of dough until it is coated. Let raise in a warm place for an hour or so. When it has doubled in size, turn it onto a lightly floured countertop and sprinkle sesame seed, flaxseed, and sunflower seeds over the flattened mass. Roll it up and knead it just enough to incorporate all of the seeds. Shape into 2 long loaves, slash tops, and pour a little melted butter over them. Let rest 5 minutes.

Bake at 350°F for about 40 minutes, until they sound hollow when tapped and are nicely browned.

JAVA RIVER CAFE
Dry Weather Creek Farm

It requires a lot of money to get into farming, and many young people do not have a lot of money. The sum of these two facts is that many young people who want to become farmers can't.

There is a solution, however, one that Mark and Wendy Lange of Dry Weather Creek Farm discovered: the Farm Beginnings program. Run by the Land Stewardship Project (LSP), Farm Beginnings offers a series of seminars and workshops for aspiring farmers. It also matches participants with seasoned farmer mentors. Wendy and Mark credit the program for their success. "It really helped us consider our options and set our goals," Wendy says. "Farm Beginnings was the driving force behind our whole operation here, and it was one of the best things we've ever done."

Patrick Moore, one of the presenters for the Farm Beginnings program, is a former LSP staffer from the Montevideo office and the founder of Montevideo's Java River Cafe. When Patrick, along with his family, set up Java River, they insisted that local foods be the focal point of the menu. At the time, Patrick never imagined that he would eventually be able to get locally milled flour for the cafe's homemade breads.

But thanks to Farm Beginnings, and a supportive community, Mark and Wendy now grow grain and mill flour on their farm near Milan. "Our area has a lot of support for our kind of farming and food production," Wendy says. "Patrick has been a

Amanda and Cathy Blaseg

great promoter of the local area and the local food system."

The Langes are building their lives as new farmers upon a foundation built by those who have labored before them — not only Patrick and LSP, but by Mark's family, who provided the land. "This farm has been in Mark's family since 1910, but it was not an active farm when we got married in 2001," Wendy says. "Farming was a new venture for both of us. We wanted to bring the farm back to life as naturally as we could, while still making it economically sustainable. I believe that having a diversity of small enterprises that fit together is the right way to go."

The Lange's idea of interlocking diversity has organic certification as its core strength. To be certified organic, a farm must be planted in a diversity of crops. In general, so as to avoid disease and insect infestations, no crop is grown on the same land for more than one year. The Langes rotate crops like flax, wheat, oats, alfalfa, soybeans, and corn over fifty acres. Since their fields are small, they don't grow very much of any one crop. That's how they became flour millers.

"We planted some certified organic crops that first year, but it was really hard to sell them," Wendy says. "Nobody wanted to monkey with 300 bushels of wheat. They wanted a container load or a semi load. I've always had an interest in making flour for bread, but I kind of had a tabletop version in mind!"

Instead of a tabletop grain mill, the Langes discovered a used stone mill in nearby Cottonwood. They bought it, disassembled the cleaner, hopper, scourer, and two stone mills, and reassembled it at their farm. "Putting the mill back together was like doing a big puzzle," Wendy says. "It was originally designed for bakers to make their own flour every day."

Out of their labors, a new product line was born: Dry Weather Creek stone-ground organic whole wheat and unbleached white flour, wheat bran, ground flax, and other products. Patrick helped the Langes place their Dry Weather Creek flour onto the shelves of Bill's Grocery in Montevideo. He also began using it in Java River's baked products.

In late 2005, Patrick left Java River to dedicate his efforts to protecting and restoring water quality and biological integrity in the Upper Minnesota River Valley watershed. Java River's new owners, Cathy Blaseg and her daughter Amanda, continue to carry on Patrick's traditions. They not only use Dry Weather Creek flour, but many other products from local farms, as well as beef from their own farm.

"Our cook, Angela, does a wonderful job," Cathy says. "She bakes a different bread every day. The oatmeal honey is to die for. She also makes specialty cheesecakes along with oatmeal scones, muffins, and cinnamon rolls to go with your morning coffee." The soup and bread of the day is the customer favorite. Angela creates a variety of savory soups, including corn chowder, beef noodle, and a stuffed pepper soup. And there's also the Bungalow Burger — made from "a recipe that has been in Montevideo since the 1920s," Cathy adds.

Cathy and Amanda, who manage the daily cafe operations, intend to continue the vision of making Java River more than just a nice cafe. "It's more of a gathering place," Cathy says. "People come and sit and talk. It's like a little haven. I hope that when people walk in the door they feel welcome and comfortable."

Cathy and Amanda are committed to nurturing local artists as well as local farmers. Java River's engagement with the arts, Cathy says, was one of the primary reasons she chose to purchase the cafe. "I'm an artist myself, and I know it's a hard way to make a living," she says. "If I can encourage people to purchase from local artists, that's great. There is a lot of talent in the area. We change the art on the walls monthly, with one show in the front and one in the fireside room." People also come to Java River to use the upstairs meeting room, an extension of the concept of the cafe as a public house.

Java River's stated goal "is to stimulate the rebirth of a new economy based on locally produced, quality foods, and creative cultural expression." Because one cafe alone may not be able to create the climate for that rebirth, the formula for that bold vision is made up of many variables. But those who are hungry for a taste of an emerging new economy can do so by enjoying bread and soup, and joining the conversation at Java River Cafe in Montevideo.

Serving up breakfast at the Java River Cafe

Wendy and Mark Lange

COUNTRY WHOLE WHEAT BREAD

If you like to bake bread, you'll love putting both of these loaves together. The dough is a baker's dream, and so tasty.

Makes 2 loaves

Proof in large mixing bowl:
1 tablespoon yeast
1½ cups warm water
¼ cup powdered milk
⅙ cup shortening
¼ cup brown sugar, packed

Mix in separate bowl:
⅙ cup ground flax
1½ cups organic whole wheat flour
½ tablespoon salt
2 to 2½ cups unbleached white flour

Proof the yeast by dissolving it in a warm liquid (sometimes with a small amount of sugar) and setting it aside in a warm place for 5 to 10 minutes until it swells and becomes bubbly. This technique proves that the yeast is alive and active and therefore capable of leavening a bread or other baked goods.

Add flour and flax mixture to the proofed mix and knead until dough is smooth, about 8 minutes. Cover and let rise in a warm place 30 to 40 minutes, and then form two loaves. Place the loaves in two 8½x4-inch greased pans. Cover and let rise an additional 30 minutes in a warm location.

Bake 35 minutes at 350°F or until loaves are golden brown and sound hollow when tapped.

CRANBERRY MULTI-GRAIN BREAD

Makes 2 round loaves

Proof in large mixing bowl:
1 tablespoon yeast
1½ cups warm water
¼ cup powdered milk
⅙ cup shortening
¼ cup brown sugar, packed

Mix in separate bowl:
⅙ cup ground flax
½ cup organic whole wheat flour
1 cup oatmeal
½ tablespoon salt
1 cup dried cranberries (Craisens)
2 to 2½ cups unbleached white flour

Add flour and flax mixture to the proofed mix and knead 8 to 10 minutes. Cover and place in a warm spot, let rise 30 to

40 minutes, then form into two round loaves. Put parchment paper on a cookie sheet and sprinkle cornmeal on the parchment; set loaves on the cookie sheet. Let rise 30 more minutes. Bake 35 minutes at 350°F or until loaves are golden brown and sound hollow when tapped.

Note: A sprinkle of coarse kosher salt on the top of the loaves before baking adds a nice contrast to the cranberries.

SAINT PETER FOOD CO-OP

Shepherd's Way Farms

Shyma O'Brien was born and raised in Saint Peter, Minnesota, but if a stranger asks him where he grew up, he won't think twice about his answer. "I grew up in the co-op," Shyma says. The "co-op" is the Saint Peter Food Co-op in the small Minnesota town of the same name.

"I've been working in the co-op for sixteen years," Shyma, now in his late twenties, says. Since Shyma's mother, Margo, has been the general manager of the cooperative since its inception, and since co-ops of the 1980s tended toward non-hierarchical work organization, it's easy to imagine a fourteen-year-old Shyma stocking shelves. When he was in his late teens, Shyma began working in the deli. Now he oversees it.

The deli offers fifty to seventy-five items, including twelve varieties of pre-made sandwiches a day. Along with the sandwiches are an array of salads — pasta, rice, fruit, and vegetable. "We have pre-pack entrees too," says Shyma, "like spinach mushroom lasagna, Creole roasted yams, and spanikopita — a spinach pie with layered filo dough, feta cheese, and lots of herbs."

The menu changes with the seasons to take advantage of fresh, local produce. "In late summer, we'll have tomato and mozzarella salad, because that's when tomatoes are in season," explains Shyma. "We get locally grown cherry tomatoes, heirloom tomatoes and fresh basil. We mix them with olive oil, salt and pepper, add fresh mozzarella, and it's fantastic."

Shyma O'Brien

Other seasonal favorites are tomato basil soup with feta and velvety yam soup with fresh dill and cream.

Shyma's strategy has been to provide foods familiar to rural and small town Minnesotans, along with more adventuresome and ethnic foods. The deli also features a range of artisanal foods from area producers. Among these are an assortment of cheeses, including five varieties of Eichten's Gouda from Center City, Stickney Hill's goat chevre from Kimball, various cheeses from Bass Lake in Wisconsin, and queso fresco, Friesago, and Big Woods Blue from Shepherd's Way Farms near Nerstrand.

Shyma knows most of the local cheese suppliers as well as many of the other vendors personally. "We are committed to supporting local sustainable agriculture," he says. But just what "committed" means took on a whole new dimension when Shepherd's Way Farms, owned by Jodi Ohlsen Read and Steven Read, experienced a devastating tragedy a couple years ago.

A few hours before dawn on a frigid January morning in 2005, the Read family was awakened by their neighbor. "He told us our barn was on fire," Jodi says. "We can't see that part of the farm from our house and by the time he called, things were pretty bad. We went out and tried to get the sheep out of the barn, but it was difficult."

The fire brought out not only the local fire department, but the neighborhood. Despite the efforts of the family, neighbors, and firefighters, the fire killed 200 lambs and 300 ewes and destroyed all of the farm's housing for sheep. The loss was not just economical, but deeply emotional. But when Steve gathered his family together later that morning and asked if anybody wanted to quit, the resounding answer was "no."

There have been times that family members have wavered since that predawn commitment. And the farm has yet to recover economically. It will be, Jodi says, a long time before the negative economic impact of the fire is no longer felt. But Jodi, Steven, and their children have persevered. They continue to shepherd and milk their sheep, and Jodi continues to make award-winning cheeses. They do this not only because of their personal will but because their community of employees, neighbors, and customers stood by them in a manner that was a testimony to their vision on how food should nurture people.

"When you have a tragedy like that it's not surprising that your family and your friends, and maybe your neighborhood and town, come and help you out and bring casseroles," Jodi says. "It's what people do. But after the fire, we understood we were part of a much bigger community. I hadn't realized how tightly knit we all are until this happened, and the co-ops and stores and restaurant owners and people who use our food came out with the most amazing support I've ever seen in my life.

"They were at our door with wonderful meals for us and our volunteers. People volunteered their time. People who had never spent any time with animals were out there helping put ointment on the sheep's burns. The co-ops took contributions from customers and helped sustain the farm. Without that kind of outpouring we wouldn't be here today." The Saint Peter Food Co-op was part of this community — providing food for volunteers and holding a fundraiser for the farm.

"One of the things people talk about a lot now is that people more and more want to know where their food comes from," says Jodi. "That can sound trite. It can sound like a marketing gimmick. But now I know it's real. People want to know the stories of the people who are responsible for their food. They want to feel connected to those people. It really showed in the response to our fire."

It was because of the support of that wide circle of friends and customers, as well as their family, that Jodi and Steven decided to take their cheeses to the American Cheese Society conference in Louisville, Kentucky, that same year. There they received four awards: their Friesago, Hope Queso Fresco Garlic Herb, Hope Queso Fresco, and Shepherd's Ricotta all received awards.

If you, by chance, find yourself carrying your tray to the spacious and sunlit seating area of the Saint Peter Food Co-op's deli, and if you have a salad with Big Woods Blue or a sandwich with Shepherd's Hope Queso Fresco, do savor the complex award-winning flavors. And know, that by nourishing yourself with that cheese, you are also savoring a wide and strong net made from threads of strong, brave, and triumphant lives.

Saint Peter Food Co-op and Deli

The Read boys: Aidan, age 15; Elia, 12; Maitias, 9; and Isaiah, 10

VELVETY YAM SOUP

A wonderfully velvety soup made with yams.
Serves 6–8

Olive oil for sautéing
2 leeks, chopped, use only white and light green
4 large sweet potatoes, peeled and sliced
1 tablespoon vegetable beef broth powder
2½ cups water
2 teaspoons dry dill weed
1⅓ cups heavy cream
1⅓ cups half & half
½ teaspoon each sea salt, black pepper, white pepper; adjust as needed

In a medium stockpot, sauté leeks in a small amount of olive oil. When leeks are tender, add the peeled and sliced yams, vegetable broth powder, water, and dill weed and simmer until all are tender.

Purée in a food processor (or blender) with the heavy cream and half & half. Heat gently in a large stock pot until warm.

Season with sea salt, black pepper, and white pepper, and serve.

Olivia gathers ripe heirloom tomatoes

CAPRESE SALAD

Use only the best quality, freshest ingredients available in this salad. A variety of Heirloom tomatoes would create a feast for your eyes — Green Zebra, Homestead, Lemon Drop, Russian Black, Brandywine. A drizzle of aged balsamic vinegar would provide a sweet finish.
Serves 2–4

4 large homegrown tomatoes, sliced
1 lb. fresh mozzarella, sliced
6 fresh basil leaves, cut as chiffonade*
1 tablespoon extra virgin olive oil
Fresh cracked pepper
Sea salt

On a tray, layer a tomato slice and then a fresh mozzarella slice. Repeat this process until the tray is full. You can start in the middle and work your way out in a spiral pattern or arrange in multiple straight lines.

Top tomatoes and fresh mozzarella with fresh basil. Drizzle with olive oil and sprinkle with black pepper and sea salt.

*To chiffonade, stack leaves, rolling them tightly, then cut across the rolled leaves with a sharp knife, producing fine ribbons.

Opposite page:
upper right: Steven Read and Jodi Ohlsen Read
bottom: Steven Read in the meadow with his flock

BLUFF COUNTRY

NOSH RESTAURANT & BAR

Rochester Farmers Market

Greg Jaworski likes to shop at the farmers' market. On any given Saturday morning during market season, Greg and some of his staff will meet at 6 AM at the kitchen at Nosh, his restaurant in Lake City. "That way we can be downtown at the Rochester market when it opens at seven," Greg says.

Seeing, touching, and smelling the freshly harvested ingredients they will use at the restaurant is a passion for the Nosh chefs. "I've told my crew that I can't pay them while we're at the market," says Greg, who has been seen burying his nose lovingly into a fresh head of fennel. "They come anyway."

Greg and his staff stroll through the Saturday Rochester market and Wednesday's Lake City market, visiting both their favorite farmers and anyone who has enticing produce. "I like working with the farmers who get excited about the things they raise, like the first carrot of the year," Greg notes.

The Nosh crew knows they'll probably find asparagus and rhubarb in the May markets and carrots in the September markets. There is a rhythm. There are also surprises and unanticipated early arrivals. For instance, the pregnant question about the arrival of the first sweet corn is conceived sometime

Greg Jaworski

around the delivery of the first tomato and the discovery of a flat of glowing golden raspberries among a dozen simmering reds.

There are times when Greg wishes Nosh was a little further down the Mississippi so he could gain some weeks of growing season. The seasonal rhythms would be more languid; less abrupt. As it is, Nosh has adopted some traditional strategies to compensate.

"We've learned to preserve things," Greg says. "I use morels we've dried in spring, and we do a lot of freezing. We'll buy a few extra flats of raspberries at the peak of the season and freeze them. We also put up strawberries."

The frozen strawberries are used in a recipe that conjures up memories of grandmothers, back porches, and summertime. "We'll have a fresh rhubarb coffee cake when we're using the last of our frozen strawberries to make ice cream," Greg says. "We use local cream and eggs for the ice cream. We'll use goat's milk to make fresh cheeses like queso blanco and queso fresco."

Nosh also turns local pork into house-made sausage. Made-in-restaurant mustard, such as cherry mustard and apricot mustard, is another house specialty. To go to the farmers' market and return to prepare mustard, ice cream, and queso blanco, and then put up raspberries, requires more kitchen time than most restaurants are prepared to give. On Saturdays, the Nosh staff is back from the market and in the kitchen by 10:30 AM.

"It's definitely more work," Greg says. "It's a difficult industry as it is. The hours are extremely long, and when we spend an additional five to ten hours a week going out in the field to find ingredients, it makes for a long week."

One of the great challenges for any restaurant is to find farmers who are prepared to sell products directly. "Several months before the restaurant opened, I spent a lot of time going out and visiting farms," Greg says. "All the terminology, like organic and free range, isn't that important to me; I wanted to see for myself how they run their business and to talk to them."

The staff at Nosh will probably never put aside their ardor for rubbing elbows with the people who grow their ingredients. However, plenty of other restaurants are unable to dedicate staff time to shopping the markets. These establishments find the Southeast Minnesota Food Network, a for-profit distribution web, to be a constructive alternative.

"We have about forty restaurant and retail accounts," says Pam Benike, a dairy farmer, artisan cheesemaker, and coordinator for the Southeast Minnesota Food Network. "We have ninety members who produce a large variety of food — everything from meat to vegetables to cheese to freshly made pies. We can provide one source for marketing, distribution and invoicing services for our members, saving farmers a lot of time

and expense."

The Southeast Minnesota Food Network arose out of a need: small farms have to compete with the large warehouses and distribution chains that large restaurant supply and grocery corporations use. That need has been affirmed by university research and think tanks in the Upper Midwest.

Residents in southeast Minnesota spent about $500 million buying food from outside the region between 1997 and 2003, according to Ken Meter of the Crossroads Resource Center. Ironically, Ken's research has shown that farmers spent about the same amount buying inputs — everything from fertilizer to baling twine — from outside southeast Minnesota. If consumers and farmers were to look closer to home for their needs, southeast Minnesota's small towns would likely experience a renaissance in the next decade or so.

There are different strategies for remaking agriculture and rural communities in southeast Minnesota. The Southeast Minnesota Food Network's collaborative distribution is one such strategy. Vibrant farmers' markets are another. The ultimate strategy for eaters, whether dining at home or at a restaurant like Nosh, is to increasingly insist on high-quality, regionally produced food.

"I feel that it's truly the way a restaurant should be," Greg says. "What our farmers are growing, or what I can find at the market, is what I can put on the menu."

GRILLED BERKSHIRE PORK LOIN WITH TWO-POTATO HASH AND ELDERBERRY DEMI GLACE

Grill a seasoned pork chop or loin approximately 4 to 6 minutes on each side, or until internal temperature reaches 140°F. (Cook times can vary greatly due to grill temperature differences and thickness of the cuts.)

Allow to rest for a couple of minutes before serving with Two-Potato Hash and Elderberry Demi Glace.

TWO-POTATO HASH
Serves 6

½ lb. bacon, small diced
3 large Yukon Gold potatoes, medium diced
2 large sweet potatoes, medium diced
1 medium sweet onion, medium diced
1 red bell pepper, small diced
1 tablespoon garlic, minced
1 tablespoon chili powder
1 teaspoon ground cumin
1 tablespoon minced fresh Italian parsley
Salt and pepper to taste

Preheat oven to 400°F. Render bacon in large sauté pan over low heat until just crispy, about 10 minutes. Remove bacon with slotted spoon and reserve. Add potatoes and onion to the bacon fat, season with spices, salt, and pepper, and sweat the vegetables for 5 minutes. Stir constantly to avoid sticking to the pan and to evenly coat vegetables with the fat and seasonings. Transfer to sheet pan and roast until the potatoes are just cooked through, about 20 minutes. Add bacon, just to reheat. Taste and check for seasoning.

ELDERBERRY DEMI GLACE
If you're unable to find elderberries, substitute blackberries or raspberries.

1 quart elderberries, cleaned and removed from stems
¼ cup sugar
3 cups good-quality beef stock

1 teaspoon kosher salt
½ teaspoon freshly ground pepper
1 tablespoon butter
Salt and pepper to taste

Cook elderberries in a small saucepan over low heat with sugar until sugar dissolves and berries wilt and burst, approximately 15 minutes. Strain through a fine mesh strainer to extract as much juice as possible while removing seeds and skins. Return the elderberry juice to pan with the beef stock and reduce the liquid to sauce consistency, about 1½ cups. Remove from heat, season with salt and pepper, and whisk in butter until it is incorporated.

GRILLED LAMB CHOPS WITH BLUE CHEESE BREAD PUDDING AND TOMATO-CUCUMBER RELISH

Season 8 to 10 lamb (or goat) chops generously with salt and pepper. Grill on each side for four minutes, or until chops reach an internal temperature of 105°F for medium-rare.

BLUE CHEESE BREAD PUDDING
Serves 6–8

1 day-old baguette, diced
6 eggs
1 quart milk
1 pint heavy cream
4 cups crumbled blue cheese
1 sweet onion
2 tablespoons minced garlic
2 tablespoons chopped parsley
Salt and pepper to taste

Preheat oven to 375°F. In a heavy-bottomed saucepan, sweat the onion and garlic in butter until soft. Add the milk and heavy cream, season with salt and pepper, and bring to a boil. Remove from heat. Place the diced baguette in a large bowl, pour the cream mixture over the bread, and stir until well mixed. Let stand for about a half an hour for the bread to absorb the milk mixture.

In a small bowl, whisk the eggs and fold into the bread mixture. Fold in the cheese and parsley. Pour into a greased 9x11" baking pan and cover with foil.

Bake for approximately 40 minutes, then uncover and continue to bake until golden brown on top, about fifteen minutes more.

TOMATO-CUCUMBER RELISH
If using cherry tomatoes, simply halve them.
Yield: 4 cups

1 pint good-quality tomatoes, different varieties if possible, diced large
1 large cucumber, or 2 small cucumbers, seeded and diced
1 lemon, juiced and zested
1 tablespoon minced fresh mint and basil
2 tablespoon extra-virgin olive oil
Salt and pepper to taste

In a bowl, add all ingredients and allow to marinate.

ROASTED BEET SALAD

This is a Nosh favorite!

6 medium beets, roots and tops trimmed
Olive oil to coat
1/2 cup pecans, chopped and toasted
1/3 cup high-quality blue cheese, crumbled

DRESSING
1 cup balsamic vinegar, reduced to 1/3 cup
1/2 teaspoon red pepper flakes
1/2 teaspoon ground cinnamon
1/2 teaspoon allspice
1/8 teaspoon cayenne

Preheat oven to 425°F. Toss beets in olive oil to coat. Place beets on a sheet tray and roast until tender (approximately 35 to 45 minutes), let cool.

Prepare dressing. Toast pecans.

When cooled, peel and cut beets into wedges. Put 4 to 5 wedges on a plate and sprinkle the pecans and blue cheese on top. Drizzle the reduced vinegar over the top. Wilted greens add nice color and flavor. This salad can be made up to a day in advance.

LINZER TART

11 oz. unsalted butter, softened

10 oz. sugar

2 eggs

1½ teaspoons cocoa powder

1 teaspoon ground cinnamon

½ teaspoon ground cloves

8 oz. cake flour

11 oz. finely ground hazelnuts

1 oz. cake flour

2 teaspoons lemon zest

10 oz. high-quality raspberry preserves

Cream the butter and sugar until light and fluffy. Add the eggs one at a time, not adding the second egg until the first egg is incorporated. Sift together the cocoa powder, the first measurement of flour, and spices. Add the ground hazelnuts and zest to the flour mixture, then add to the creamed butter and mix until just incorporated. Weigh out 18 oz. of the dough and mix in the second amount of the flour. Reserve this dough at room temperature.

Place the remaining dough (without the added flour) in a pastry bag with a small plain tip and pipe out the dough over an 11" tart pan, starting at the outside edge, making concentric circles to evenly cover the pan. Try to use all the dough to achieve the correct thickness of crust.

Bake at 375°F for about 15 minutes or until the crust just starts to color. Remove from oven and cool slightly. Spread the preserves evenly over the crust, leaving a 1/4" border around the outside.

Place the remaining dough in the pastry bag with the same tip. Pipe straight parallel lines, about a half inch apart, across the tart. Then pipe a second set of lines across the tart at a 45 degree angle to the first set.

Bake again at 375°F for about 25 minutes, or until there is a nice golden brown color on top; check frequently. Cool the tart before eating.

This tart will actually benefit by being made up to a day ahead for best flavor and results, since the nuts in the dough will absorb moisture from the air and most importantly the jam, making for a moist pastry.

DANCING WINDS
FARMSTAY RETREAT

Callister Farm

"When we get close to going to market, it's like getting ready for a performance," says Lori Callister, a farmer from the Northfield area who is a vendor at the Midtown Global Market with her husband, Allen. "I get really pumped up. Where else in the world can you get a job where people tell you they need your product so badly? If I didn't have that customer contact, I don't think I could continue. It's like an elixir."

Mary Doerr, proprietor of Dancing Winds Farmstay Retreat, is a neighbor to the Callisters. "I use to make artisan goat-cheese," says Mary, "but cheesemaking was a little isolating for me. One of the reasons I was able to transition out of cheesemaking is because the farmstay was growing. I really enjoy the social aspect of it, and creating a safe haven for people. I also like to expose people to goats. I guess that's ultimately my mission."

Mary and Lori's agricultural projects emerged from a long history of neighboring during a time of immense creativity and change in southern Minnesota's agricultural scene. Mary's vision, which continues to evolve, was born from the flames of tragedy.

"I started milking goats in September of 1985," Mary recalls, "but I had a barn fire a year and a half into it and lost the barn and a lot of the goats." But the fire sparked her inspiration for building the cheese plant, which eventually transformed into her bed and breakfast venture.

Mary Doerr

Among those who were there to provide Mary fortitude, as she gathered up the ashes of her barn and charred goats, was Ken Taylor. Mary remembers how Ken was himself a guiding light to her and so many others as he forged the now widely shared vision of an inextricable link between urban and rural people.

During the early 1980s, while Ken Taylor was creating the Minnesota Food Association, a coalition of urban and rural citizens working towards a sustainable food system, the Land Stewardship Project and Nature Conservancy were bringing together some of the best and brightest farmers of southeastern Minnesota to form the Sustainable Farming Association. It was within that farmer-driven organization that Lori and Mary first collaborated.

"We were both on the board of directors of the Sustainable Farming Association's Cannon River Chapter," Lori remembers. "When our family first joined, about 1990, it was because we were committed to raising crops and poultry without chemicals and antibiotics."

"It was fun because we had creative people like Dave and Florence Minar, Dan and Muriel French, Mary Doerr, and Mike and Linda Noble," Lori says, recalling some of the pioneers in Minnesota's movement toward a new agriculture. "We were very active with field days and learning from each other. There

were a lot of interesting things going on."

The Minars and Frenches led the way in grass-fed dairying. The Minars now run Cedar Summit, one of the premier on-farm dairies in the country where they make outstanding milk, cream, yogurt, and ice cream. The Frenches are part of a small cooperative that produces the nationally award-winning Pastureland butter. The Nobles are leaders in direct-marketing sustainably produced pork, chicken, and more recently, lamb.

Mary and Lori have blazed their own trails as well, but like the others, continue to collaborate. A few years ago, when Lori was still making her own handcrafted jams and jellies, Mary served the jeweled creations to her bed and breakfast guests. Today, Mary gets her preserves from Mary Ellen Frame, another Sustainable Farming Association contact. And since the Callisters have become full-time chicken, turkey, and egg producers, Mary's guests also enjoy the Callisters' poultry products. Mary doesn't cook breakfast for her guests, rather she stocks the refrigerator in her farmstay with fine local ingredients that guests can use to make their own meals.

"I get a lovely seasoned chicken sausage from the Callisters," Mary says. "My guests who are meat eaters love that." The Callister family makes a wide range of sausages, which come in bulk, links, and patties, from their chickens.

"I use all my own recipes," Lori says. "We make an herb sausage, an Italian sausage and an apple-maple sausage, using local apples and maple syrup. We get the syrup at the Saint Paul Farmers' Market from Mark Christopher, who is from Spring Valley, Wisconsin. We get cranberries for our cranberry sausage from another Wisconsin farmer at the market. It started out as a turkey sausage because I wanted something that tasted like Thanksgiving dinner, and it evolved to chicken. We also have a savory mushroom and wild rice sausage. We get our wild rice at the farmers' market, as well."

Mary doesn't participate in sausage production on the Callister farm, but every Wednesday, in exchange for fresh poultry, she helps butcher and package chickens. But Mary doesn't go to butchering day just to earn a few drumsticks.

Lori Callister

"It takes ten or twelve of us to process poultry," Lori says. "At noon, we have a big meal together. It's a nice social hour for everybody, mostly neighbors and friends. Even when we butcher, there's a lot of socializing."

As part of this extended community, Mary earns not only chicken and eggs, but bragging rights. When she stocks her guests' refrigerator and cupboards with food from the Callisters, Frenches, or Mary Ellen Frame, she's likely to share stories that go along with the food.

"I want to promote the sustainable farmers who are nearby," says Mary. "I want to promote the good products that people are making and raising. And while it allows me to be on a soapbox a little about sustainable agriculture, I'm very careful not to jam anything down their throats. I'm a bit more subversive; I believe I can get to them through their stomachs.

"It's really fun to be able to say, 'this butter is from grass-fed cows,' and the reason it's so marvelous is because those cows are on fresh grass getting lots of exercise and sunshine."

In fact, Mary's entire farmstay experience, modeled after European-style farmstays, is pretty low key. Guests can cook and eat according to their own schedule and rhythm. They can sleep in or get up early and go bird watching. They can walk the meditation maze that Mary maintains. They can help with chores or milk a goat — or they can just commune with the goats.

"Goats are incredibly affectionate animals," Mary says. "They are friendly, lively and, like a cat, demand affection on their own terms. They are also comical. They'll come up to the fence and want their ears scratched. In the summer I welcome people to put plastic over their boots and just sit in the pens with the animals. Some of my favorite guests come at least for a couple of the seasons. The husband enjoys bird watching while his wife relaxes in the barn, where the goats form a line to get brushed."

Knowing that people take that kind of pleasure in her beloved goats is an elixir for Mary, just like visiting with customers at the Midtown Global Market is a tonic for Lori Callister.

CHEVON MEAT LOAF

Serves 6

2 lbs. ground chevon (goat meat)
1 cup tomato juice
1 small onion, finely diced
1 carrot, diced
2 eggs
1½ cups dried breadcrumbs
1 teaspoon dried sage
Salt and pepper to taste

Mix all ingredients together. This should be a bit moist as chevon is a very lean meat. Turn the mixture into a greased loaf pan. Cook at 400°F 1 to 1½ hours, or until a knife comes out clean. You can add a ketchup glaze on top of the loaf during the last 15 minutes. Serve with candied yams.

ASPARAGUS WITH GOAT CHEESE AND MORELS ON FETTUCCINE

Serves 4–6

½ cup shallots, minced
2 tablespoons unsalted butter
½ cup dry white wine
½ cup chicken broth
½ lb. fresh morels or other brown mushrooms, such as porcini, sliced crosswise
½ cup heavy cream
8 oz. mild goat cheese (about 1 cup)
¾ lb. asparagus, trimmed, cut into ½-inch pieces, cooked in boiling salted water for 2 to 3 minutes, or until tender, but still bright green
¼ cup fresh chives, minced
¾ lb. fettuccine

In a heavy skillet, cook the shallots in butter over moderately low heat, stirring until softened; add wine and simmer the mixture until the wine is reduced by half. Add the broth and the morels and simmer the mixture, covered, for 10 minutes or until the morels are tender. Add the cream and the goat cheese and cook the mixture over low heat, stirring until the cheese is melted. Stir in the asparagus, chives, and salt and pepper to taste. Keep the sauce warm.

In a kettle of boiling water, cook the fettuccine until it is *al dente*. Drain it well, and toss the pasta with the sauce in a bowl.

HERB GOAT CHEESE QUESADILLAS

Serves 8

1 lb. chevre (fresh goat cheese)

½ cup low-fat milk

1 tablespoon fresh basil, chopped

1 tablespoon fresh cilantro, chopped

1 tablespoon fresh parsley, chopped

1 tablespoon fresh sage, chopped

8 flour tortillas

½ cup olive oil

Preheat oven to 375°F. Combine goat cheese and milk in a bowl. Mix together and add the fresh herbs. Spread ¼ cup cheese mixture onto each flour tortilla and fold in half. Brush tortillas with olive oil and place on a baking sheet. Bake for 8 to 10 minutes or until golden brown. Cut each in half and serve warm.

CALLISTER'S BEER CAN CHICKEN

1 farm-fresh chicken, ¾ to 1 lb. per person

1 teaspoon granulated garlic

1 teaspoon paprika

1 teaspoon cinnamon

1 teaspoon black pepper

1 teaspoon oregano

1 teaspoon sage

1 teaspoon sea salt

1 teaspoon onion powder

½ can beer

Mix spices together and rub mixture on outside of chicken. If you have a roasting stand for the chicken, use it. It holds the bird upright and allows the juices to drip down into the pan. Place the pan in the oven or on the grill first. Pour beer into the bottom of the cooking pan. Place the chicken into the pan. Bake for about 20 minutes per pound at 375°F. Juices will run clear when done. A thermometer placed in the thigh of the chicken should read 180°F. You can also pour the beer directly into the cavity, if desired.

THE BACKROOM DELI

Dream Acres

"Most of the people who work here started out as customers," says Andy Denny, a co-founder of the Backroom Deli, a little vegetarian restaurant in the back of the Good Food Store Cooperative in Rochester. "They enjoyed the food and atmosphere so much, they applied for jobs."

The Backroom Deli tends to build this kind of loyalty in its customers. And the feeling is mutual for Andy. He likes his customers. He likes them individually. He likes them as a group. And he takes delight in their diversity.

"Our customers are really diverse and I think that's what's neat about us," he says. "You'll have businessmen sitting next to punk rockers. You've got your hippies that come here as well as local TV anchors."

That diversity, Andy believes, makes The Backroom Deli an epicenter for plots, plans, and events throughout the Rochester community. "A lot of things grow out of our deli. It's not just people who are vegetarian, but all kinds of people meet here to plan things."

So is it the food? The ambiance? The wait staff? It is likely that all of the above come together to form a whole that is greater than a sum of the parts. But since it is a cafe and delicatessen, the food is a weighty consideration. The fact that it's

Andy Denny

all vegetarian makes it unique. Andy figures the Backroom Deli is one of very few of its kind in Minnesota.

Vegetarianism is important to Andy. He is against killing and eating animals, or using animal products in any way. It was with that in mind that the storeroom at the Good Food Store was turned into the Backroom Deli. Food free of animal products was, and is, the guiding principle of the place. But vegetarianism at the Backroom Deli is a back-room matter. Customers aren't proselytized. They are served top-notch food made "from scratch" using recipes developed by Andy and the staff. Diners are nourished on food like hearty winter stew served with an onion dill roll made by Rochester's own Bread Baker Company.

"What the customers' personal views are doesn't play a big role here," Andy says. "Most people do eat meat, but people who want some great organic food come here. They simply enjoy the good food."

The effect of that good food is measurable satisfaction from vegan and non-vegan alike. For five years running, *Rochester Magazine*'s readers have awarded the Backroom Deli first place for the best health food. To cast their votes readers, of necessity, had to be satisfied and gratified customers.

So, yes, the food it is. They come, and come back, for the food. But the wait staff and ambiance nourish the clientele also.

Waiters, Andy says, enjoy visiting with the customers. And at the Backroom Deli everybody, the entire staff of eight, is wait staff.

"Everybody that works here does everything," Andy says. "They cook, wash dishes, prep food and wait on customers. Everybody likes to wash dishes and everybody likes to talk with the customers."

The deli's celebration of equality establishes a social ambiance. But the brightly colored mural on one of the walls, created by a former employee, of course, deepens and widens the sense of generosity provided by the staff. The mural is of a woman surrounded by a plenitude of fruits and vegetables. The world is good, it proclaims.

There is other art. Andy and the staff are dedicated to creating a space for local artists to exhibit their work. There has been a new show every two months since the deli was founded in 2002.

There is, of course, another type of art on display at the Backroom Deli. Whether it's the spicy spelt burger, Cajun tofu wrap, or a peach mango smoothie, the art of the top-quality ingredient is prominent. The best vegetarian ingredients are organic and locally produced, according to Andy. And, although the best is not always to be had, the Backroom staff is ceaselessly seeking and striving for it via their vendors.

One of their favorite suppliers is Whole Grain Milling Company. That Welcome, Minnesota, family-owned farm and milling company provides the deli with organic corn chips, along with garbanzo and black beans. Another favorite supplier is DreamAcres, owned by Todd Juzwiak and Eva Barr.

With their two sons, Todd and Eva run a thirty-member subscription vegetable business. In a beautiful basin near Spring Valley, they till their fields with oxen, making the already pastoral setting more so. The farm also has horses, sheep, chickens, and a dog.

In addition to growing an array of vegetables, Todd and Eva host a variety of workshops on their farm through Tillers International. Timber framing, maple sugaring, and blacksmithing are among the offerings. Eva is active in the theater and brings this love and expertise to a special summer program she has developed. Flourish is a week-long summer camp for young people that links performing arts, dance, music, theater, puppetry, and agriculture in a total immersion educational experience on the farm.

"I admire everything they do," says Andy. "They live on a turn-of-the-century farm, grow organic produce and are 'off the grid,' meaning they use minimal electricity, and what they do use they generate themselves. They're really nice people and I'm always glad to see them when they come by."

Todd and Eva are also part of the community that encouraged the creation of the Backroom Deli. They are part of the Vegetarian Information Group of Rochester, or VIGOR. Andy met them at one of VIGOR's monthly potluck dinners.

"When we were thinking of starting The Backroom Deli, we knew we had a good set of customers already in the VIGOR potluck group," Andy says. "Twenty to thirty people come to the potlucks every month. Seventy to a hundred people come to our annual Thanksgiving dinners."

VIGOR, like the Backroom Deli, is an epicenter of activity and ideas in Rochester. In addition to the monthly meals and Thanksgiving dinner, the group is also a food vendor at Rochesterfest, where they sell their specialty barbecue vegetarian riblets.

The VIGOR potlucks, although regularly scheduled, create only a transitory and mobile space for the nurturance of community. But it was that mix of activism, friendship, and celebration at VIGOR that helped inspire Andy, who was the bulk foods buyer at the Good Food Store, to clean out a storage room and create a permanent community gathering place. And there people eat and meet. Customers become employees who greet and feed other customers. Farmers bring beautifully grown ingredients and artists hang brightly colored paintings. And the whole stew of the community bubbles and simmers. There are circles of friendship and nurturance. And good things come to life.

BACK ROOM DELI SALSA

This is a colorful salsa that's even good during the winter.
Yield: 4 cups

2 to 3 ripe fresh tomatoes, diced; or one 28-oz. can diced tomatoes (Muir Glen Fire Roasted Diced Tomatoes are good when fresh tomatoes aren't in season)
1 to 2 jalapeños, small diced
1 carrot, peeled and small diced
1 medium onion, small diced

1 medium bell pepper, small diced
1 tablespoon lemon juice, or juice from half a lemon
2 tablespoons fresh cilantro
1 teaspoon sea salt
1 teaspoon black pepper

Mix all ingredients and serve. Will keep refrigerated for one week.

BACK ROOM DELI HUMMUS

Enjoy with chips, pita bread, or in a wrap. A mini meat grinder works great for mashing the beans.
Yield: 2 cups

⅛ cup water
⅛ cup lemon juice, or juice of ½ large fresh lemon
4 cloves garlic, minced
1 to 2 tablespoons olive oil
¼ cup tahini
Pinch of cayenne

1 tablespoon minced onion
1 teaspoon sea salt
1 cup dry chickpeas, cooked, or one 14.5-oz. can chickpeas

In a blender, blend the water, lemon juice, and garlic. Pour the juice mixture in a bowl and add the olive oil, tahini, and spices. Mash the beans in a separate bowl or use a mini meat grinder. Add the beans to the tahini sauce mixture and stir to combine.

SCANDINAVIAN INN

Hilltop Pastures Family Farm

The Scandinavian Inn and the Hilltop Pastures Family Farm suit each other well. "We met Peter Torkelson at a Lanesboro Chamber of Commerce meeting," Sara Austin, of Hilltop Pastures, says. "Peter said he might be interested in some of our eggs and pork products and invited us to come by for a visit. My husband and I are committed to building local relationships and selling our food directly to our customers."

That kind of thinking has a strong appeal to Peter Torkelson, who runs the Scandinavian Inn with his wife, Vicki, and is a retired employee of the Minnesota Pollution Control Agency. Peter prefers a lifestyle that allows him to walk and bicycle, rather than drive.

"My goal is to have the inn make as small of an ecological footprint as possible," he says. "We call ourselves an environmentally sensitive bed and breakfast. That means we buy locally as much as we can and serve organic produce when we can. We use natural cleaning products and soaps. We use no synthetic chemicals or fertilizers on our lawn, mow with a back-powered reel mower and clear our sidewalk with a shovel."

Peter and Vicki have been innkeepers since 2004. During that time, they have developed a sense of what an environmentally sensitive inn is. Although Peter says the concept is evolving, part of it is simply living in a town where he and his

Peter Torkelson

guests can walk the few blocks to Lanesboro's picturesque downtown. Some of the other practices they've put into place include providing cloth napkins at breakfast, brewing shade-grown, fair trade coffees, line-drying towels and linens outdoors when the weather permits, and buying local and organic foods.

So when Peter had the opportunity to serve Sara and Tom Austin's eggs in a portabello mushroom dish, he was more than happy to do so. He was particularly charmed that the shells came in three colors: blue, brown, and white.

Sara, who left her job at the Mayo Clinic in 2004 to raise a family and, along with her husband Tom, become a farmer, is excited for the opportunity to fill that gap for the Torkelsons and others near her farm.

The philosophies of the Austin and Torkelson families align in terms of being environmentally sensitive in how they run their respective businesses. The Austins have adopted a system written about extensively by Virginia farmer, Joel Salatin, that rotates cattle, pigs, and chickens on pastures. It is a "beyond organic" system that maximizes the health of the animals, grasses, and soil.

If you visit the farm, you will see pigs happily rooting in the mud, cows grazing on rolling pastures, and chickens pecking away at the grass in their portable pens. "When the grass is green, the chickens are always outside," says Sara. "They love it."

The Scandinavian Inn is just one of the bed and breakfasts in town that have this commitment to buying locally grown foods. Down the street at the Cady Hayes House, Peggy Hanson will also serve you farm-fresh eggs and vegetables from her husband Frank's garden. And if your timing is right, you may also get morels or other wild foods that Frank has foraged from the woods around Lanesboro.

In fact, the commitment to local foods ripples throughout this small community of less than a thousand people. Up the road at the Eagle Bluff Environmental Learning Center, community members and visitors can come to "Dinner on the Bluff," the first Saturday of most months. Here guests partake in a delicious gourmet meal made with local ingredients, followed by a presentation from a noted speaker.

So come to town to bike or ski the miles of trails, canoe down the Root River, or shop in the charming stores. Pick up a Green Routes brochure and explore unique and interesting places in the area. Stay at the Scandinavian Inn, Cady Hayes House, or one of the other bed and breakfasts in town. And ask about the stories behind the food you are being served.

*Tom and Sara Austin and their children
Shane, Sami, and Caleb*

Breakfast at the Scandinavian Inn

NORWEGIAN ROMMEGROT CREAM PUDDING

Serves 6–8

½ pound butter (2 sticks or 1 cup)*
½ cup white flour**
1 quart half & half***
2 tablespoons sugar
½ teaspoon salt (or slightly less)

Melt butter (reserve ¼ cup) in a large pan. Lightly sauté flour in the butter over medium-low heat. At the same time, heat half & half in saucepan over medium-low heat until it is shiny on top or until scalding. Scalding temperature is 150°F. If a skin develops on top of the cream, remove it before proceeding.

Add hot half & half slowly to flour and butter mixture, stirring constantly. Never reverse direction. (I use a flat whisk because I prepare the butter-flour mixture in a large sauté pan.) Add sugar and salt once all half & half has been incorporated. Keep stirring until the Rommegrot comes to a boil. Pour Rommegrot into a heat-safe bowl, or pour into a crock pot set on low.

To serve, pour reserved ¼ cup of melted butter on top and serve Rommegrot warm. This approximates the traditional method of preparing and serving Rommegrot. At the Scandinavian Inn we often serve the Rommegrot at room temperature, with no melted butter on top and sprinkled with cinnamon and sugar.

Note: I have had success dividing this recipe in half and even in fourths.

* If you don't wish to serve Rommegrot with the reserved ¼ cup butter on top, begin with only ¾ cup (1½ sticks) of butter.

** Since my usual organic white flour is a little bit heavier than commercial flours, I often take out 1 teaspoon or so of flour so the pudding will not get too thick.

*** Equal parts of milk and heavy (whipping) cream can be substituted for half & half.

DANISH RØDGRØD RASPBERRY PUDDING

Serves 4

½ lb. fresh raspberries
About 1½ cups water
2½ tablespoons cornstarch
6½ tablespoons sugar
½ tablespoon lemon juice
Pinch of salt
Whipped cream

In a medium saucepan, combine berries and water. Bring to a boil, simmer for 5 minutes. Strain out seeds and save liquid. (I first force them through a colander or other coarse strainer, then through a fine strainer, then through a cloth.) Discard seeds. Add enough water to make 2 cups of liquid and return to the saucepan. Add lemon juice.

Combine dry ingredients in a measuring cup or small bowl, stirring thoroughly to blend cornstarch and sugar. Slowly add spoonfuls of the liquid and stir until a thin paste results.

Bring liquid to 185°F or a very low simmer, and pour the paste into the liquid, stirring constantly with a wire whisk. Maintain the temperature and stir with whisk for about 5 minutes until thickened to a jelly-like consistency. Cover and cool for a few minutes. Pour into 4 sherbet glasses. (If pudding has skinned over, stir with whisk before transferring to sherbet glasses.) Refrigerate.

Serve cold with a dollop of whipped cream on top.

VEGETARIAN QUICHE

Serves 8

PIE CRUST

1 cup whole wheat flour (we use pastry flour)

⅓ cup cold butter

3 to 5 tablespoons cold water

In a mixing bowl, cut cold butter into flour until pea-sized balls are formed. Add water, one tablespoon at a time, until dough is moistened and workable. Roll dough or press into a 9-inch glass pie pan to form the bottom crust.

Liz says, "I tend to have difficulty getting all of the dough evenly moistened. After I have removed and pressed into place the workable part of the dough, I tend to add more water to the drier flour that remains in the bowl. I usually make the pie crust while the cooked vegetables are cooling."

QUICHE FILLING

5 eggs

1 cup milk

2 cups cheese, shredded; use a mix (we typically use equal amounts of mild cheddar, sharp cheddar, and Monterey Jack)

1 large onion, chopped

1 small-to-medium head of broccoli

1 cup sliced mushrooms

About 1 to 2 tablespoons dried tomatoes, broken into small pieces

Cooking oil

1 teaspoon dried rosemary

1 teaspoon dried sage

½ teaspoon dried parsley

½ teaspoon dried leaf marjoram

½ teaspoon dried basil

¼ teaspoon black pepper

Peel and coarsely chop onion. Cut up broccoli (head and stem) into about ¾-inch pieces. Drain mushrooms.

Measure out herbs into a coffee cup or other small bowl. (Fresh herbs can be used as available. We typically use chopped fresh basil, sage, and parsley from our garden but usually add some dried sage with the fresh. Use about three times the amount of fresh to dry herb.)

In a large frying pan, fry onions for about one minute in oil, add mushrooms and continue to fry until onions begin to brown, then add chopped broccoli and cover for one minute. Uncover, stir in herbs and continue to fry for 30 seconds. Remove from heat and add dried tomato pieces. (We usually freeze the dried tomatoes, then remove them from the freezer and quickly crush them with our hands while they are still frozen and brittle.) Cool.

Sprinkle a layer of shredded cheese in the pie shell. Remove the broccoli heads from the frying pan and evenly spread those over the cheese. (Do this to ensure that the broccoli flowers are buried within the quiche. If they are on the top and exposed to the heat, they will burn.) Sprinkle some of the remaining vegetable mix onto this layer. Add a layer of cheese, a layer of vegetables, a layer of cheese, and finish with a layer of vegetables on the top.

Add milk and eggs in a bowl, and mix. At this point you can pour the egg/milk mixture into a covered container, cover the quiche, and refrigerate both overnight. Combine them the following morning just prior to baking. Pour eggs and milk into pie shell.

Baked uncovered in a 350°F preheated oven for 75 minutes. Remove from oven and allow to stand for 5 to 10 minutes before serving.

TWIN CITIES AREA

RESTAURANT ALMA AND BRASA

Otter Creek Growers

"What I'm doing isn't a trend," says Alex Roberts, owner of Restaurant Alma. "At least as far as I'm concerned it's not. The only way I know how to cook is with seasonal foods. I prefer local ingredients if available because local farmers produce the best food. If the level of quality puts me in a higher price range, I'm OK with that. I grew up with food from the garden, good whole foods, and that's what I serve."

Working with food that's as fresh as possible and controlling it in its natural state is the way Alex works. No par-baked bread or mixes. "Society is very accepting of processed food, and in fact, they trust food that's in a package. Somehow it's 'cleaner' because it's packaged and has a pretty label. The perception is that a local farm can't provide that level of safety, and it's just not true," Alex says. "Others think that 'food is food.' Just because you can eat it, doesn't mean it's food."

Some of Alex's favorite customers are those in their seventies and eighties. "They'll come in and say, 'This is the way I remember food tasting when I was a kid,'" he explains. "That's because that food came right off the farm or from the garden just like the food we use here."

As a hands-on restaurateur — and father of young children — Alex doesn't travel much these days. But he does credit his time in New York and Florence for providing a good base for what he does. In those places, he learned to work with fresh ingredients and with constantly changing menus.

Alex Roberts

At Restaurant Alma, Alex likes to have a mix of the old and the new on his menu. "When I'm developing a menu, I look at what's available," he says. "Since my dad farms, I know when specific crops are at their peak and I structure my menu from there. We always have red meat, white meat, fish, shellfish, and vegetarian choices on the menu, so there's enough variety for everyone." Even if crab is on the menu, you can feel comfortable that it was a "good" purchase. Alex will only buy seafood caught using sustainable practices and from areas that aren't overfished.

"I've worked with many of the same suppliers for years," Alex comments. "Dave and Florence Minar of Cedar Summit Farm provide me with exceptional dairy products. My dad's stuff (Otter Creek Growers) is on par with anyone's. I don't bounce around a lot. My suppliers are planning on my order and I stick with them."

Alex's new restaurant in northeast Minneapolis, Brasa, is less upscale than Restaurant Alma but includes many of the same seasonal, local ingredients. Here, he focuses on more universal foods — rotisserie chicken, slow-roasted pork, red beans and rice, corn, braised greens, grits, and sweet potatoes. "Food is the best medicine," Alex says. "It's the things you have to include in your diet, not what you need to avoid, that is important. That's the way it has been for most of the history on this planet. I like to think what I'm doing is normal."

FENNEL GRATIN

3 cups fennel bulb, sliced
1½ cups leeks, white part only, sliced
1 cup sweet onion, diced small
Zest of one orange
2 cups fennel cream (recipe below)
1½ cups coarse-grated Parmesan cheese

Mix together fennel, leeks, and onion with salt and pepper. Place half of the vegetable mixture in a lightly greased 9x13-inch pan. Top with half of the Parmesan cheese and orange zest. Top with remaining leek and fennel mixture. Pour the fennel cream to almost cover vegetables, and top with other half of cheese. Cover with foil and bake at 350°F to 375°F until vegetables soften, about 25 minutes. Uncover and bake until lightly browned.

FENNEL CREAM

2½ cups cream
1 piece star anise
1 tablespoon fennel seed
½ yellow onion, rough chopped
Salt and white pepper to taste

Combine ingredients and simmer until reduced to 2 cups.

SWEET CORN FLAN

Serves 6
3 cups fresh corn kernels
Butter, for sautéing
Toasted and ground cumin, salt, tumeric, and white pepper, to taste, for seasoning
½ cup cream
7 egg yolks
Truffle oil, for seasoning
Pinch of tumeric

Sauté the corn gently with a nub of butter, cumin, white pepper, salt, and a pinch of tumeric; remove from heat when softened. When corn has cooled, blend with cream, yolks, and truffle oil. Strain this mixture through a fine chinois and pour into prepared molds (8 oz. ramekins) coated with non-stick spray. Bake in a water bath at 350°F for 40 to 50 minutes or until just set.

SEASONAL GREENS SOUFFLE

Serves 12

2 lbs. fresh chard
¼ cup unsalted butter
¼ cup reconstituted porcini mushrooms, chopped
¼ cup fontina cheese, or mild-flavored melting cheese, diced
2½ cups bechamel sauce (recipe below)
3 eggs, separated
Salt and pepper

Cook greens, in just the water clinging to the leaves after washing, for 5 minutes. Drain, squeezing out as much water as possible, and chop. Gently sauté the greens in butter for 5 to 7 more minutes; remove from heat. Allow to cool, then stir the greens, porcini, and fontina into the bechamel sauce, then stir in egg yolks one at a time. Beat the egg whites until stiff peaks form. Gently fold in beaten egg whites into cheese sauce. Pour mixture into prepared molds (8 oz. ramekins). Bake in a water bath of simmering water at 350°F for 30 to 40 minutes, or until set.

BECHAMEL SAUCE

¼ cup butter
¼ cup all-purpose flour
2 cups whole milk
Salt and pepper
Pinch of nutmeg

Melt the butter in a pan over medium heat, whisk in the flour until incorporated, then add milk, whisking constantly until it comes to a boil. Season with salt, lower the heat, and cover and simmer gently, stirring occasionally for at least 20 minutes. Remove from heat; adjust seasoning with pepper, nutmeg, and more salt if needed.

BRYANT LAKE BOWL, BARBETTE, AND RED STAG

Moonstone Farm

Rewards come in many different ways. It doesn't get much better than when you're able to act on a desire to make a difference and actually see it happen. When Kim Bartmann opened Bryant Lake Bowl (BLB) in 1993, she set forth to create a venue with a relaxed atmosphere, affordable prices, and good food. This funky restaurant/bar meets bowling alley meets cabaret theater became a quick success in the Uptown neighborhood.

But a few years ago, Kim had a crisis of conscious with her job. She says, "I already had a strong value system for providing healthy food, but I wanted to align some of those healthy food values with better environmental practices." Inspired by a Business Alliance for Local Living Economies conference she attended, Kim set out to be more environmentally responsible in her restaurants.

"First off, I made the decision to get as much sustainably and locally grown food as possible for our menu," Kim says. "This means less fuel is used in transporting food, the land is better cared for by those using sustainable farming practices, and more money stays in the local community." With the opening of Barbette in 2001 and the Red Stag in 2007, Kim is able to expand her impact in the community and on the landscape.

Kim only hires chefs who share her mindset. "I've hired a forager to strengthen and seek out partnerships with additional growers. There's a need to know what a grower can consistently

Kim Bartmann

get for us, and how quickly they can ramp-up for additional needs or ventures," Kim says. "We also need to look at how new products can be worked into our menu."

Beyond buying food from local farmers, Kim also is committed to educating others. BLB highlights a different producer each month on their menu, and customers gets to "meet the farm and the face" behind the food. For instance, they might meet Audrey Arner and Richard Handeen from Moonstone Farm in Montevideo, who provide the grass-fed beef for the burgers at BLB. The steaks she gets from them are featured on the menu at Barbette. Audrey and Richard are part of Pride of the Prairie, a network for local, sustainable farmers in western Minnesota.

At her new restaurant, the Red Stag, Kim has gone a few steps further. The building is the first LEED-certified restaurant in the state, meaning it incorporates green technologies into its design and operation. Kim also has a van that will pick up products from smaller farms. And this won't be just any van, it will run on vegetable oil from the restaurant fryers. Good for the environment, good for the farmers, good for BLB, Barbette, and Red Stag.

Kim says, "Yes, we are preaching to our customers, but most of them want to know where their food comes from. While the idea of local or organic is still a bit of a barrier for some people, we overcome that."

Audrey Arner and Richard Handeen

CHICKEN WINGS IN BARBECUE SAUCE

This barbeque sauce is used on BLB's organic, free-range chicken wings from Larry Schultz Farms. BLB roasts the chicken wings ahead on a cookie sheet at 375°F for about an hour. When ordered, they are grilled and then tossed in a pan with the sauce. Deliciously spicy and so good with the Black River Blue Cheese Dressing (below).

Yields about 5½ cups

1½ cups brown sugar
½ cup butter
¾ cup white vinegar
1 cup ketchup

One 5 oz. bottle Heinz 57 sauce
1 tablespoon whole celery seed
1 cup diced yellow onion
¼ cup Sriracha chili sauce (this garlic hot sauce can be found at many large grocery stores or Asian markets)
1 tablespoon lemon juice

In a saucepan, caramelize butter and sugar on medium heat until bubbly. Add vinegar and whisk until lumps are gone. Add all the other ingredients and simmer on low heat until thickened. Cool and refrigerate in an airtight container. Holds for about one week.

DIJON MUSTARD VINAIGRETTE

BLB serves this dressing on its Star Prairie (Rainbow Springs) smoked trout and beet salad.

Yields about 3¼ cups

½ cup Grey Poupon Dijon mustard
2 tablespoons champagne vinegar
1 cup fresh lemon juice
2 tablespoons dried thyme
½ teaspoon kosher salt
½ teaspoon cafe coarse-ground black pepper
1 cup extra virgin olive oil
½ cup honey

Mix mustard, vinegar, lemon juice, thyme, salt, and pepper in a food processor or a bowl. Slowly add olive oil to create an emulsion while running food processor or whisking continuously. Then slowly add honey in the same way.

Put in airtight container and store in the refrigerator. Holds about one week.

BLACK RIVER BLUE CHEESE DRESSING

The Black River Blue Cheese from Wisconsin is perfect in this dressing, tangy yet mild enough for those who don't like blue cheese. This will become your favorite dressing, as a dip or on a salad. BLB also uses this dressing on its organic grilled bison salad (Silver Bison Ranch) and on its organic grass-fed mushroom and blue cheese burger (Moonstone Farm).

Yields about 2 cups

1 teaspoon minced garlic
⅓ teaspoon (or to taste) ground black pepper
⅔ teaspoon (or to taste) white pepper
⅓ teaspoon (or to taste) dry ground mustard

1 tablespoon white wine vinegar
⅓ cup plain yogurt
⅓ cup sour cream
⅓ cup mayonnaise
2⅓ tablespoons buttermilk
⅔ cup blue cheese crumbles
4 tablespoons minced parsley

Mix all ingredients well in a bowl. Store in airtight container in the refrigerator. Holds for about one week.

BAYPORT COOKERY

Thousand Hills Cattle Company

*I*f health-conscious chefs and consumers were to place an ad for beef, it might look something like this: *Wanted: One-hundred-precent grass-fed cattle produced on paddocks using no synthetic pesticides or fertilizers. Only British breeds need apply.*

"The bottom line is it just tastes better," says Jim Kyndberg, chef and owner of the Bayport Cookery, a gem of a restaurant located in the beautiful St. Croix River Valley. "I'll put a grass-fed steak alongside a grain-finished steak any day. And if you put organic milk, cream, or ice cream alongside conventionally produced products, you'll see how much better it tastes. It's a world apart."

Jim Kyndberg

Jim serves grass-fed beef that comes from Todd Churchill's Thousand Hills Cattle Company in Cannon Falls. Todd has done his homework when it comes to producing top-quality grass-fed beef. "For the most nutritious, tasty, and tender beef, you've got to be discriminating," asserts Todd. This boils down to an important factor: the breed.

"The British breeds do best on grass," Todd says. "The Continental breeds take too long to mature. If you buy grass-fed beef in France, it's from three- or four-year-old animals. The meat is tough and requires special cooking."

British breeds include some familiar names — Hereford, Black and Red Angus, Shorthorn, and Galloway — and the not-so-familiar Devon, British White, and Murray Grey.

Continental French breeds include Charlois, Simmental, and Limosin, among others.

So why do we have a British versus Continental French controversy? "Up until the mid-century, cattle-herd genetics in the United States were almost all British breeds," Todd explains. "They are genetically predisposed to eat grass. They put on a lot of fat early and mature early, without ever being fed any grain."

But a shift happened in the 1960s and 1970s that brought about the development of feedlots and grain-fed cattle. That was when the U.S. Secretary of Agriculture urged farmers to plant fence row to fence row and dramatically increase the production of crops like corn. "Raising all that corn and feeding it to cattle in confined feedlots worked very well from an industrial agriculture model," explains Todd. "You got more beef faster. But it didn't work with the British breeds. They got fat too quickly. So the feedlot owners started asking for crossbred cattle. Now ninety-five percent of the cattle in this country are cross breeds with Continental genetics."

Grass-fed proponents have a list of reasons why raising cattle on grass is favorable. Among these is research that indicates that grass-fed beef is healthier because it has higher amounts of the beneficial omega-3 fatty acids.

Jim Kyndberg doesn't buy Thousand Hills beef only because it's tasty and healthy. He also likes to buy from his neighbor, Fresh and Natural Foods in Shoreview, who supply Jim with the beef. Fresh and Natural began ordering from Thousand Hills because they recognized the superior quality. "I really like how these relationships develop in sustainable agriculture," Jim says. "I like that I get beef from a guy my neighbor knows and trusts."

Not that Jim isn't willing to go the extra mile to connect with his suppliers. His interest in a community-based food supply began years ago, shortly after he had his bags packed for cooking school in San Francisco — and then a call to an internship with a Cayman Islands restaurant lured him away. In that "hot hole," as he describes the kitchen he worked in for six and a half days a week, he fell in love. The romance, which has endured, was with what he calls the "motion poetry of the kitchen" and the preparation of the freshest, best ingredients.

"On Grand Cayman, I was blown away by the people who would show up with fish in their truck," he says. "They were going out in a little row boat and sometimes coming back with 100 pounds of snapper. I was amazed that they could catch them and be at the back door of the restaurant that day."

When he moved from Grand Cayman to a Florida restaurant, Jim was chagrined to learn that although surf still rumbled within earshot, fresh seafood wasn't available. So he started going to the docks to get to know the fisherman. "One day I bought a 200-pound marlin, put it into my Toyota Corolla, and hauled it to the restaurant," he recalls.

Now in the Minnesota heartland far from the beaches, Jim is still the kind of hands-on chef who likes to dig into the harvest. "I find it very fulfilling to go out and work on a farm that will bring vegetables to me next week," he says.

Jim goes to great lengths to ensure fresh and locally produced ingredients grace his menu selections. In springtime, his menu may feature forest-harvested morels or fiddleheads; in autumn, harvest-themed selections. Bayport is famous for its three-, five-, and nine-course meals served in an elegant, warm setting. "We pay a lot of attention to detail and put a lot of thought and creativity into what we do," Jim says. "We are a small restaurant; to be competitive, we have to create menus you can't find anywhere else."

Todd Churchill

WILD ACRES PHEASANT WITH WILD RICE RISOTTO AND DRIED CHERRY PINOT NOIR SAUCE

Remove the breast meat from three pheasants; be careful to reserve as much skin as possible. Season the breast with salt and pepper. Sear breast, skin-side down, in a hot sauté pan with 1 tablespoon of olive oil. Brown on both sides and finish cooking in a 350°F oven until cooked through, less than 10 minutes. Remove from the oven and let the meat rest, covered, for at least 5 minutes before slicing.

WILD RICE RISOTTO

1 shallot, minced
2 cloves garlic, chopped
2 tablespoons clarified butter
1 cup chicken stock
1 cup heavy cream
2 cups cooked wild rice
$^1/_2$ cup grated Parmesan cheese
2 tablespoons chopped Italian parsley
Fresh salt and pepper to taste

Sauté the shallot and garlic in the butter in a medium saucepan until soft. Add the stock and cream, reduce by half. Add the wild rice and simmer. If too thick, add a little more stock. Remove from heat. Stir in the Parmesan cheese and parsley. Season with salt and pepper.

DRIED CHERRY PINOT NOIR SAUCE

$^1/_2$ cup dried cherries
$^1/_2$ cup chicken stock
$^1/_2$ cup red wine (preferably Pinot Noir)
2 tablespoons balsamic vinegar
1 tablespoon maple syrup
1 to 2 tablespoons unsalted butter
Salt and pepper

Over medium heat, mix together and reduce the stock, wine, vinegar, and cherries to a syrupy consistency, about 15 minutes. Lower the heat and stir in the butter. Season to taste.

ASSEMBLY

Place a scoop of risotto in the center of the plate, slice the pheasant into four equal pieces, and fan around the rice. Drizzle with sauce and garnish with seasonal vegetables.

BEEF TENDERLOIN WITH GARLIC CONFIT, WILTED SPINACH, AND BRAISED OXTAIL

Serves 8–10

Trim a 3- to 4-lb. Thousand Hills Cattle beef tenderloin of all silver skin and excess fat. Season the beef with salt and pepper. Place the meat on a hot grill or pan and sear on all sides until golden brown. Place in a roasting pan into a preheated 400°F oven and cook to an internal temperature of 125° for medium rare (about 12 to 15 minutes per pound). Remove the meat from the oven, cover with foil, and let rest at least 15 minutes before slicing.

OXTAIL PREPARATION

Season 2½ lbs. of oxtail with salt and pepper. Sear in a hot sauté pan with olive oil until golden brown on each side. Place the seared meat in a roasting pan or heavy casserole dish. Add 1 chopped medium onion, 1 chopped large carrot, 2 ribs of chopped celery, 2 bay leaves, and a sprig of fresh thyme. Pour 2 cups red wine and 3 cups beef stock over the meat and vegetables. Cover the pan with foil and slow-cook in the oven at 285°F for at least 6 hours, or until the meat is fork-tender. Strain and save the braising juices.

GARLIC CONFIT

Peel all cloves from 2 heads of garlic and place in sauté pan with 1 cup of extra virgin olive oil. Place on medium heat and cook the garlic until it begins to brown. Remove from heat and add fresh herbs: thyme, rosemary, and parsley, to taste. Cover pan and place it in a 285°F oven for approximately 1 hour.

ASSEMBLY

Clean the meat from the oxtail and shred. Place the oxtail meat in the sauté pan with the garlic confit and 2 cups (firmly packed) fresh spinach. Warm over medium heat until the spinach has wilted. Slice beef tenderloin into desired portions and top with the oxtail mixture. Place a portion of the garlic and spinach alongside the beef. Spoon some braising juices on the side.

BIRCHWOOD CAFE

Riverbend Farm

Birchwood Cafe owner Tracy Singleton explains it this way: "We're not just *in* the neighborhood, we're *for* the neighborhood."

That neighborhood is the Seward area of Minneapolis, where it's easy to concur with the cafe's website description of what you'll find: "A crossroads of hot food and cool comfort, Birchwood Cafe is one part funky coffee house, one part neighborhood cafe, and two parts eclectic organic kitchen." The cafe's motto is "Good Real Food," and everything on the menu typifies this slogan in the most creative way.

Before opening Birchwood, Tracy waited tables at Lucia's — owned by Lucia Watson, one of the region's best-known local-foods advocates. When she opened her own restaurant, Tracy was able to continue to work with many of the same local vendors. For Tracy, the rewards come not only from serving good food, but from supporting small, local farmers who are critical to a healthy food system.

A hefty amount of the produce on Birchwood's menu comes from Greg Reynolds at Riverbend Farm in Delano. Whether discussing the upcoming crops, paging through seed catalogs, or on a field trip at the farm picking beans and radishes, Tracy and her staff garner a lot of inspiration from this relationship. "Each season Greg asks, 'What can I grow for

Tracy Singleton

you?'" Tracy says. "And my thought is always, how can I best showcase his beautiful food?"

Tracy truly values the personal nature of these relationships. It is the part of her job she loves most. "I really appreciate the opportunity to chat with my farmers and producers. They are the face of our food. Victor Mrotz from Hope Creamery, Pat Ebnet from Wild Acres, and the Hilgendorf family from Whole Grain Milling, we all face similar challenges of running a small business according to our values," Tracy says. She loves the summer deliveries, these hardworking farmers with their children in tow, happy to be helping out. "I always send them off with a cookie or lemonade or a loaf of rye bread made with the flour specially milled to our bread baker's specifications," she says. These relationships are at the core of Birchwood Cafe's "good real food."

When Tracy bought out her former business partner in 2004, the internal reorganization that was required gently forced her into thinking about what she was doing and why, and helped to solidify her mission and values. "At heart, the Birchwood Cafe is about connectedness and relationships," she says. "Basically, we are building community through food. We live in such a fragmented world. Cooking with local seasonal ingredients helps ground and connect us to the earth. This lends a sense of respect for the ingredients we use and an appreciation for the food we eat which connects us to each other and our community."

Tracy likes being the connection point for her customers and farmers. She says, "When you have that connection with a sense of place, and you know where your food comes from, I think we're all better for that."

Greg Reynolds

ROASTED PUMPKIN HAND PIE

Birchwood uses Riverbend Farm's Cinderella pumpkin or sunshine squash, as well as cipollini onions, when available. They choose aged goat cheese from Mount Sterling, Wisconsin.

Serves 8 as a main course; 12 to 16 as an appetizer

FILLING

1 medium sweet pumpkin or butternut squash
¾ lb. aged goat cheese, coarsely grated
2 lbs. cipollini onion, roasted
¾ cup olive oil
¾ cup white wine
4 bay leaves
2 sprigs fresh thyme
2 tablespoons peppercorns
Salt and pepper, for seasoning

Cut pumpkin into wedges. Oil and season; roast in 350°F oven just until cooked through, about 45 minutes. In roasting pan, mix onions with olive oil, white wine, bay leaf, fresh thyme, and peppercorns; cover with foil and roast 15 to 20 minutes in

375°F oven. Mix cheese with onions and pumpkin. Season mixture with salt and pepper. Set aside, prepare dough for crust.

CRUST

8 oz. cream cheese
1 cup unsalted butter, Hope Creamery preferred
½ tablespoon salt
2 cups flour

The butter makes all the difference in this pastry, which is why Birchwood always uses Hope Creamery unsalted butter. Beat butter and cream cheese until combined. Add flour and salt and mix until a smooth dough ball is formed. Cut into 6 equal pieces and roll into balls. Using a rolling pin on a floured surface, roll out dough to make about an 8-inch circle. (Make smaller circles if you are making this as an appetizer portion.) Scoop filling onto the middle and fold edges up over the filling. Brush with cream and cook in 375°F oven for 20 to 30 minutes, or until golden brown.

This is served at Birchwood with a simple watercress and Granny Smith apple salad, tossed in a light champagne vinaigrette.

FARRO CARROT CAKES WITH FENNEL KUMQUAT PISTACHIO SALAD AND CARROT COULIS

Farro is the ancient Italian grain from which all others derive. It is similar to spelt but with a firm chewy texture. The success of French farmers supplying the grain to elegant restaurants has sparked renewed interest in farro. Choose packaged farro carefully to make certain you are getting *Triticum dicoccum* (farro's Latin name).

6 cups farro; or wheat berries or spelt

3 cups cannellini beans or other white beans

2 tablespoons olive oil

1 bulb garlic

3 cups shredded organic carrots

3 oz. flour

½ tablespoon cumin

½ tablespoon ground ginger

½ tablespoon salt

¼ tablespoon pepper

2 tablespoons lemon juice

Rinse farro and cook until tender, about 30 minutes. Use 3 parts water to 1 part grain. Check every ten minutes to avoid overcooking. The farro should not split open. This is a sign that you have overcooked the grains.

Cook cannellini beans, or other white beans, and cool. Using a food processor or food mill, purée to a smooth, light consistency with extra virgin olive oil and garlic. Shred carrots to finest consistency with a food processor or box grater. Combine grains, bean mixture, carrots, and remaining ingredients and mix thoroughly.

Fry on griddle till just browned. Serve with Fennel Kumquat Pistachio Salad and Carrot Coulis (recipes below).

Farro Carrot Cakes can be made up to two days in advance and kept refrigerated. Reheat in oven to serve.

FENNEL KUMQUAT PISTACHIO SALAD

2 bulbs fennel, shaved or thin julienne

6 kumquats

¾ cup toasted pistachios

Red wine vinegar

Olive oil

Salt and pepper to taste

Combine shaved or julienned fennel, thinly sliced kumquats, and toasted pistachios in a bowl. Drizzle lightly with vinegar (you can always add more, but you can't take away), olive oil, salt, and pepper. Toss lightly, and arrange on the plate.

CARROT COULIS

3 medium-sized carrots, peeled and uniformly diced

1 small yellow onion, julienned

1 clove garlic

4 basil leaves

3 cups vegetable stock

Salt and pepper to taste

In a small saucepan, lightly sauté carrots, onion, and garlic until onions are transparent. Use low heat and do not caramelize the vegetables. Add basil, and cover with vegetable stock. Simmer for 3 to 4 minutes, remove from heat and purée in a blender. Adjust taste with salt, pepper, and a small dollop of extra virgin olive oil. Serve sauce at room temperature.

STRAWBERRY RHUBARB COBBLER

Delicious served with a drizzle of Cedar Summit cream or a scoop of ice cream. Birchwood uses seasonal strawberries through Footjoy Farm or Southeast Minnesota Food Network; rhubarb through Riverbend Farm, when in season; cornmeal from Whole Grain Milling, Welcome, Minnesota; and unsalted butter from Hope Creamery.

Serves 8–10

FILLING

3 pints strawberries, quartered
2¼ lb. rhubarb, cut into ½-inch pieces
3 tablespoons cornstarch
1½ cups sugar
½ teaspoon cinnamon
1 big pinch nutmeg

Toss fruit into cornstarch, sugar, cinnamon, and nutmeg. Pour into 9x13-inch greased pan. Bake at 400°F for 40 to 50 minutes, or until fruit is bubbly around the edges and juices are thickened and clear. Prepare topping while fruit is baking.

TOPPING

1½ cups flour
½ cup yellow ground cornmeal
½ cup sugar
1 tablespoon baking powder
¼ teaspoon salt
6 tablespoons cold, unsalted butter, cut in pieces
¾ cup heavy cream

Combine dry ingredients. Add butter and cut in until the mixture has the consistency of coarse sand. Gradually add cream until dough pulls together. Break off pieces and spread evenly over fruit. Return to oven and bake for 25 to 30 minutes until golden brown.

CORNER TABLE

Southeast Food Network

Corner Table is as cozy as it sounds — a cheery neighborhood eatery that offers both comfort foods and classics. In this Kingfield neighborhood restaurant, chef-owner Scott Pampuch serves up dishes that are simple, yet divine. Just watching Scott prepare a quick staff breakfast of sliced pork hock, eggs, and an apple and potato hash will make you grab onto a fork and beg for a bite. How could such simple ingredients be so good?

That's one of the guiding philosophies behind Scott's success. "Good food doesn't have to cost a fortune and it doesn't require exotic ingredients," he says. Scott works to provide exceptional value along with exceptional flavor — like that found in the braised pork ribs, the hand-cut pasta, or the French toast and apples.

The Southeast Minnesota Food Network is an important source of ingredients for Scott. It also is a neighborly thing. Having grown-up in Winona, the Network gives him the opportunity to support those

Scott Pampuch

Pam Benike

in and around his hometown. More than ninety regional producers, with products ranging from dairy and vegetables to meats and honey, work under a set of guiding principles that emphasize sustainability, land stewardship, and fair prices.

Scott's question to his suppliers is always, "What are you long on?" Pork loin is always in demand, but by being flexible, Scott is able to further support local farmers and challenges his own creativity at the same time. You could say that Scott has the "whole pig" philosophy when it comes to creating his menus. One night it's chops and hocks, the next night loin and bacon . . . right until the pork is, well, down to the bone. And then it's soup! "That's how I grew up. My uncle had a butcher shop and I learned how to use it all," Scott says.

"As a chef you realize so much of cooking is not the recipe you start with, but how you make it your own," Scott explains. "It's how you add your own blend of seasonings and, more importantly, the energy you put into it."

SPRING LAMB WITH ORANGES, LEMONS, GREEN OLIVES, AND OVEN-ROASTED POTATOES

This lamb is also very good when cooked on the grill if weather permits.

2 large oranges

1 large lemon

$\frac{1}{3}$ cup brine-cured green olives (preferably Italian)

4 large garlic cloves

$\frac{1}{4}$ cup packed, fresh, flat-leafed parsley leaves

4 tablespoons olive oil

3 lbs. Yukon Gold boiling potatoes

7 lb. leg of lamb (ask the butcher to remove the pelvic bone and tie lamb for easier carving)

With a vegetable peeler, remove zest from oranges and lemon; reserve lemon and orange. Pit olives. In a food processor fitted with steel blade, finely chop zest, olives, garlic, and parsley with 2 tablespoons oil.

Preheat oven to 400°F. In a large roasting pan, arrange lamb and with the tip of a sharp small knife, cut small slits all over lamb. Rub olive mixture over lamb, pushing it into slits. Halve reserved lemon and squeeze juice over lamb. Season lamb with salt and pepper and roast in middle of oven 20 minutes.

Reduce temperature to 350°F. Peel potatoes and cut into $1\frac{1}{2}$-inch pieces. In a mixing bowl, toss potatoes with remaining 2 tablespoons oil to coat; season with salt and pepper. Add potatoes to the roasting pan, around and/or under the lamb. Loosen potatoes from pan with a metal spatula and turn occasionally. Continue cooking 1 hour more, or until a meat thermometer inserted into thickest part of meat registers 135°F and potatoes are tender and browned. Transfer lamb to a cutting board and let stand while making gravy. Transfer potatoes to a large bowl and keep warm.

PAN SAUCE

$\frac{1}{2}$ cup dry white wine

$\frac{1}{2}$ cup chicken stock

Whole lemon and oranges, quartered

$\frac{1}{2}$ tablespoon all-purpose flour

$\frac{1}{2}$ tablespoon unsalted butter

Add wine, chicken stock, and orange and lemon quarters to roasting pan and deglaze pan over moderately high heat, stirring and scraping up brown bits. Transfer mixture to a small saucepan and bring to a boil. In a cup with your fingers, blend together flour and butter. Add flour mixture into sauce, whisking until incorporated, and simmer gravy, stirring occasionally, for one minute. With a slotted spoon, remove any potato pieces from sauce, strain, and serve over or alongside the lamb.

EL NORTEÑO

Whole Farm Co-op

Clemen Serna and Estella Guintana, partners in the Mexican restaurant El Norteño, are just doing what comes naturally. "That's how we grew up. We went out to the garden to pick our food, and that's what we ate," says Clemen.

Home for the sisters, before 1990, was Chihuahua, Mexico. "We grew up in a small town; we would grow our own vegetables and eat what was fresh. We know what is good for you," Clemen continues. "And then, ten years ago when we started the restaurant, we met a wonderful man, Tim King. Tim introduced us to many local growers so we could continue with what we know."

Clemen Serna and Estella Guintana

Many of the growers Tim introduced the women to are part of the Whole Farm Co-op. The co-op includes more than thirty farm families in central Minnesota who are committed to growing food sustainably. On a regular basis, Whole Farm delivers everything from fresh produce, meats, and cheese to flour and honey to customers in the Twin Cities. Their customers include members of churches, colleges and nonprofits, as well as food co-ops and several restaurants. El Norteño is the only restaurant they supply that serves authentic Mexican fare.

Clemen and Estella buy a number of ingredients from Whole Farm Co-op, which they use in their entrees. They lament that it is sometimes hard to get the peppers they need because of Minnesota's short growing season. "It is especially hard to get all your products locally in the winter," says Clemen, "but we do what we can." In the summer, they rejoice in getting fresh cilantro from the garden. "It is so tasty and smells so good," Clemen says.

The food at El Norteño is delicious and the setting friendly and unpretentious, just like Clemen and Estella. It is all made from scratch — the enchiladas, tamales, and chile rellenos, as well as rice and beans. The tortillas, both corn and flour varieties, are always fresh. "If you know what fresh food is, you know the difference, you can taste it," says Clemen. "We know what fresh Mexican food tastes like, and we make it here."

ENCHILADAS SUISAS

Serves 4–6

1 tablespoon vegetable oil
$\frac{1}{2}$ lb. tomatillos (husks removed), chopped
1 small onion, chopped
1 garlic clove, minced
4 jalapeño peppers, chopped (the seeds and membrane are
the hottest part of the pepper; remove it for a milder sauce)
10 corn tortillas
2 cups shredded chicken
$1\frac{1}{2}$ cup Chihuahua cheese
1 cup chicken broth
Sour cream, chopped onion, and cilantro, for garnish

To prepare the sauce, simmer tomatillos, garlic, onion, and peppers in vegetable oil for 10 minutes. Process the mixture in a blender (or use an immersion blender) until smooth. Add salt to taste.

Preheat oven to 350°F. Place less than $\frac{1}{4}$ cup chicken and 2 tablespoons cheese in the center of each tortilla. Roll up and place, center seam down, in a 9x13-inch baking dish. Repeat, using all tortillas and chicken. Pour enchilada sauce over all, sprinkle with additional cheese, and bake for 30 minutes.

Garnish with sour cream, cilantro, and raw onion.

GARDENS OF SALONICA

Hill and Vale Farm, Zweber Farm, Roger's Farm

Sixteen years ago, Anna Christoforides' mother said, "Why are you opening a restaurant *there*? No one will find you!" Many people have found the Gardens of Salonica in northeast Minneapolis, including the restaurant reviewer Zagat, who named the Gardens the second-best Greek restaurant in the nation in 2004. That's a lot of great moussaka.

Anna and Lazaros Christoforides have always been co-op members and use organic, local products personally. But while starting a family and working on their graduate degrees at the University of Minnesota, they couldn't always afford meat. Anna created a vegetarian moussaka — no meat in the budget that week — that inspired Lazoros to exclaim, "People will beat a path to your door for this!" And it's still one of the favorite selections on the current menu.

From student housing to an Uptown Art Fair booth to a shared restaurant kitchen for their growing catering business, in 1991 the Christoforides found an unoccupied building in northeast Minneapolis that was available with one year's free rent. With that bonus, and a full year of painting, removing three layers of linoleum, plastering, and creating the artsy decor — no Mediterranean murals on these walls — they opened with seven tables. That was the beginning of the Gardens of Salonica that you see today.

Anna Christoforides

While centuries-old Greek cuisine is the basis of the menu, Anna carefully updates dishes and puts her own twist on things. A customer favorite — boughatsa — is one of these. Greek food lovers will recognize the concept as that found in spanikopita or tyropita — phyllo pastry filled and baked with tasty ingredients. Among the varieties of boughatsa at Gardens of Salonica are leek-skordalia, mushrooms with kefalotyri cheese, and on the sweet side, custard and apricot.

The secret to the food at Gardens of Salonica is the same secret known by all great cooks Greek and non-Greek alike — fresh, wholesome ingredients. There is barely a food-service ingredient used at the restaurant. Hill and Vale Farm in Wykoff and Zweber Farm in Elko provide the meat. All eggs, sugar, and butter are organic, from free-range animals. The herbs and produce come from Roger's Farm. The co-ops provide the honey; the coffee is free-trade Borealis. And the local farmers' market on Larpenteur is a favorite seasonal stop.

Do people realize the effort Anna goes to in order to provide this quality of food? "Probably not," she says, "but just come for the Greek food and you'll realize that something different is happening here."

FASOLAKI ARNI (LAMB AND GREEN BEANS)

Serves 4–6

LAMB

2 lbs. all-natural lamb, suitable for braising (bone-in shoulder or ribs)

2 tablespoons olive oil

6 to 10 cloves garlic, sliced

1 cinnamon stick

½ teaspoon salt

½ teaspoon black pepper

1 cup tomato sauce (or fresh tomatoes; see note)

Heat Dutch oven on medium high, add olive oil, and sear all ingredients together except tomato sauce, stirring constantly until browned.

Reduce heat. Add 1 cup tomato sauce (or in summer when tomatoes are ripe, cut 4 tomatoes on the hemisphere, squeeze out and discard seeds, and grate tomatoes over meat until only peel is left. Discard peel.)

Cover and reduce on a very low flame. Stir periodically to ensure that all the meat cooks in contact with the tomatoes. Cook about an hour or until the meat falls off the bone. Remove from heat. Cool.

GREEN BEANS

4 dry white onions, sliced to make 6 cups

2 bay leaves

1 teaspoon dry organic basil

1 teaspoon salt

1 teaspoon black pepper

2 lbs. fresh green beans with trimmed ends; or frozen green beans, at room temperature

2 cups fresh diced skinless tomatoes

In a separate Dutch oven, heat ½ cup pure olive oil. Cook onions with all the spices until they are translucent.

Add the green beans and stir, cooking the beans until they just start to turn from bright green to army green. Then add the tomatoes. Cover and reduce heat until desired texture of the beans is reached. Greek cooks tend to cook beans until they are very soft.

ASSEMBLY

Lift lamb and tomatoes out of the Dutch oven with a slotted spoon and add to green beans. Simmer an additional 10 minutes until flavors blend. Adjust salt and pepper to taste.

Serve with crusty peasant bread and chunks of feta.

TOURLOU

Delicious hot or at room temperature.

Serves 4–5

½ cup extra virgin olive oil

2 medium onions, sliced

1 small fennel bulb with fronds, sliced (discard leaves)

¼ cup sliced garlic

½ teaspoon salt

½ teaspoon black pepper

¼ cup fresh basil, chopped (or 1 teaspoon dry basil)

2 bay leaves

4 cups eggplant, cubed

4 cups zucchini, cut into 1-inch rounds

4 cups green beans (with ends trimmed)

2 cups tomatoes (fresh chopped or canned sauce)

Preheat oil in large sauté pan or Dutch oven. Add onions, fennel bulb, and seasonings. Sauté until onions wilt. Add garlic. Continue sautéing until onions and garlic are soft and transparent. Add eggplant, stirring to coat with oil and seasonings. Cook about 5 minutes, stirring periodically. Add zucchini and green beans. Stir to coat. Reduce flame/heat to medium low and cover.

Cook until green beans start to change color (bright green to army green). Add tomatoes; stir in gently. Cover and simmer until cooked to preference.

Serve with feta and crusty peasant bread.

RIZOGALO (RICE PUDDING)

Serves 4

1 quart organic 2% (or whole) milk

½ cup uncooked jasmine rice

1 cinnamon stick

1 teaspoon organic lemon zest

Heat to simmer over medium high, stirring frequently. Simmer and stir until slightly thickened and rice rises to surface and stays (about 30 minutes). Add scant ½ cup organic sugar. Heat additional 5 minutes. Cool and serve.

HEARTLAND
Cedar Summit

Heartland owner, Lenny Russo, won't try to force feed his way of doing things on anyone. But when he does express himself — which he'll do quite freely — it's fun to partake in the feast of how and why he cooks the way he does.

Heartland, which Lenny co-owns with his wife, Mega Hoehn, originated from a desire to feature North American Midwest cuisine, using ingredients made by artisan producers or raised by small family farmers who use either organic or natural farming methods. Lenny explains, "When you're a chef, you're relating to people in the most fundamental way, giving them sustenance. You bear a certain responsibility to give them healthful food. I take that responsibility seriously, and the connection to how the food is produced goes right along with that responsibility."

Lenny Russo

A meal can get someone's attention pretty quickly, and customers often ask Lenny about the food he is serving them. He takes pleasure in telling them about the ingredients and what farm a tomato, or the cream, or a cut of meat came from. Lenny says, "I started putting a lot of the provenance of the ingredients on the menu and, now, if I leave that information off, customers ask where the food came from."

Lenny's standards are high. "If a farmer shows up with a bag of beans at my door, I'm not necessarily going to buy them, I want to know *how* they're grown," he says. "You have to be a farmer with some integrity to work with me. I'm always asking the questions. . . are you rotating your crops? Are you grazing your animals? And how are they treated?"

Lenny likes buying from Hill and Vale Farm because he knows that owners Joe and Bonnie Austin are careful to nurture biodiversity on their rolling pastures near Wykoff. He likes Thousand Hills Cattle Company, not only because of their high-quality beef, but because the small company is playing an important role in bringing like-minded farmers together to meet a growing demand for pasture-raised beef.

Working as partners with his farmers and producers is vital to a sustainable relationship. Sometimes a small farmer will need more for his product than a larger farm would need. Some chefs can't afford to do that. If a chef is working for someone else, part of the job is to maximize profits. Lenny wants to pay the price that allows the farmer to get his product to the restaurant, make a living, and support the farm.

"Of course, when you're chef-owner, your measure of success is different than someone that wants to make a lot of money," Lenny says. "My measure of success is that all the bills are paid and there's money in the bank. In my case, this is what I do and how I fulfill myself. I don't need to get rich because I'm rich just being here."

Lenny has a national reputation as a purist — as owning a restaurant that represents the best of the Midwest might indicate. He says, "I don't know why people come here. They may be interested in my issues, they may like the food, or they may just live around the corner and it's a convenient place to eat, but hopefully, they leave with the message and are satisfied.

MIDWESTERN CASSOULET

Lenny suggests using Kramarczuk's Polish ham sausage, called Krakovska, or any good garlic pork sausage. Kramarczuk is located in northeast Minneapolis.

COOKED WHITE BEANS

1 lb. great northern white beans, rinsed and checked for stones
1 smoked pork hock (½ lb. smoked bacon, diced into ¼-inch chunks, may be substituted)
1 sweet onion, peeled and studded with cloves
1 large carrot, peeled
1 bouquet garni consisting of 2 parsley sprigs, 2 thyme sprigs, 1 bay leaf, 2 garlic cloves, and 15 black peppercorns

Soak the beans overnight, making sure there is twice the water as there are beans by volume. Drain and place in a pot with the other ingredients. Pour in enough cold water so it is again twice the volume of the beans. Bring the pot to a boil over high heat. Reduce the heat to a simmer, and gently cook the beans until they are tender but not splitting (about 1½ hours).

Drain the beans, making sure to reserve the cooking liquid for further use. Remove the vegetables and the bouquet garni. Turn the beans out onto a sheet pan and allow to cool. Separate the meat from the pork hock; discard the bone. Return the meat to the beans.

RAGOÛT

2 lbs. sweet onions, peeled and diced into ¼-inch pieces
10 garlic cloves
½ cup rendered duck fat (or rendered pork fat or whole unsalted butter)

4 lbs. lean pork, diced into ¼-inch chunks
2 lbs. white wine garlic sausage, cooked and bias sliced
2 lbs. Cooked White Beans (recipe above)
½ gallon brown chicken or meat stock
(or equal amount of reserved bean cooking liquid)
2 cups reserved bean cooking liquid
4 Roma tomatoes or 2 large tomatoes (must be ripe), peeled, seeded, and chopped
2 tablespoons tomato paste
1 each bouquet garni consisting of 2 parsley sprigs, 2 thyme sprigs, 1 bay leaf, and 1 whole nutmeg
1 tablespoon sea salt
1 teaspoon Tellicherry black pepper, freshly ground

Brown the onions and garlic in the duck fat in a shallow, non-reactive saucepot or brazier (5-quart shallow saucepan, 6x14-inch) over medium high heat. Add the pork and sausage. Cook for ten minutes until the pork is well browned; add the beans. Pour in the stock and the reserved cooking liquid. When the ragoût begins to simmer, stir in the tomatoes and the tomato paste. Add the bouquet garni and season the ragoût with the salt and pepper. Cover the pan and continue to simmer for one hour. The ragout may be cooled and served at a later time at this point. This will allow time for the flavors to blend.

To serve, spoon some of the ragoût into an oven-safe baking crock. Top generously with fresh bread crumbs and dot the top with some small knobs of rendered fat or whole unsalted butter. Bake in a 400°F oven until the cassoulet begins to bubble. Remove and serve immediately.

FRESH VEGETABLE SLAW

Serves 6–8

⅓ lb. Savoy cabbage, cored and thinly sliced
⅓ lb. red cabbage, cored and thinly sliced
⅓ lb. fresh fennel bulb, cored and thinly sliced
⅓ lb. turnips, finely julienned
⅓ lb. table carrots, peeled and finely julienned
⅓ lb. sweet onions, thinly sliced
1 cup grapeseed oil

⅓ cup apple cider vinegar
¾ tablespoons fine sea salt
1½ teaspoons Tellicherry black pepper, freshly ground
3 tablespoons fresh flat-leaf parsley, chopped
3 tablespoons fresh tarragon leaves, chopped

Combine all of the ingredients in a non-reactive mixing bowl. Toss well, making sure all of the ingredients are well blended.

ASPARAGUS-BARLEY RISOTTO

This dish may be served as an accompaniment for chicken or fish or may be served as a vegetarian entrée.

Serves 6–8

1 quart Court-Bouillon (recipe below); you may also use organic vegetable or chicken stock
2 tablespoons grapeseed oil
1 white onion, peeled and diced into ⅛-inch pieces
1 carrot, peeled and diced into ⅛-inch pieces
2 ribs celery, peeled and diced into ⅛-inch pieces
1 clove garlic, minced
½ lb. hulled barley
2 cups asparagus, bias cut and blanched
1 tablespoon fresh thyme leaves
2 tablespoons unsalted butter
¼ cup fresh Parmesan cheese, grated
1 teaspoon fine sea salt, or to taste
½ teaspoon black pepper, freshly ground, or to taste

Bring the bouillon to a slow simmer in a non-reactive pot. Meanwhile, heat the grapeseed oil in a shallow braising pan or saucepan over medium-low heat. Add the vegetables and garlic and lightly sauté until tender. Add the barley and season it with the salt and pepper. Sauté the barley with the vegetables until it begins to change color, stirring occasionally with a wooden spoon. This is called pearlizing.

Once the barley is pearlized, slowly add the bouillon using a four-ounce ladle. Continue to stir the barley as you add the stock. Allow the stock to become completely absorbed before adding another ladleful. Repeat this process until all of the stock is used. The barley should be tender but not soft.

Add the asparagus and thyme and remove the risotto from the heat. Continue to stir gently until the asparagus is warmed through. Gently stir in the butter and the cheese and adjust the salt and pepper if necessary.

COURT-BOUILLON
Yield: 1 gallon. Preparation time: 2½ hours

2 white onions, peeled and diced into ¼-inch pieces
3 carrots, peeled and diced into ¼-inch pieces
½ stalk celery, peeled and diced into ¼-inch pieces
1 medium leek, cleaned and diced into ¼-inch pieces
1 garlic bulb, quartered
2 tablespoons grapeseed oil
1 cup dry white wine
1 bouquet garni consisting of 2 thyme sprigs, 2 marjoram sprigs, 3 parsley sprigs, 1 bay leaf, 5 whole allspice, 10 white peppercorns, 10 black peppercorns, and 12 fennel seeds

In a stock pot over moderate heat, sweat the vegetables and garlic in the grapeseed oil until tender. Add the white wine and the bouquet garni. Fill the pot with one gallon of cold water and bring it to a boil over a high flame. Reduce the heat and simmer for two hours, skimming intermittently. Strain through a fine mesh strainer lined with moistened cheesecloth.

Florence and Dave Minar

GREEN GAZPACHO WITH DILL SOUR CREAM

Know your peppers! Early season jalapeños may be too mild, and late-season peppers may be too spicy. This is a well-balanced sweet-and-spicy dish — don't overdo it.

GAZPACHO
1 cup honeydew melon, peeled and seeded
1 tablespoon jalapeño peppers, gilled and seeded
¼ cup green bell peppers, gilled and seeded
¼ cup green onions, chopped
½ cup cucumbers, seeded and chopped
1 cup tomatillos, husked and chopped
1 cup sweet onions, peeled and diced into ¼-inch pieces
2 tablespoons Banyuls vinegar or other red wine vinegar
2 tablespoons fresh Italian parsley, chopped
1 tablespoon fine sea salt
½ teaspoon white pepper, freshly ground

Purée the fruits and vegetables with the remaining ingredients in a high-speed blender until smooth. Transfer to a labeled container with a tight-fitting lid and refrigerate immediately.

DILL SOUR CREAM
1 cup sour cream
2 tablespoons fresh dill, chopped
½ teaspoon sea salt, or more, to season to taste
½ teaspoon Tellicherry black pepper, freshly ground

Mix all of the ingredients thoroughly in a stainless steel mixing bowl until well blended.

To plate, ladle six ounces of gazpacho into a chilled serving bowl. Garnish with sour cream and some freshly chopped chives.

HELL'S KITCHEN AND HELL'S KITCHEN DULUTH

Silver Bison Ranch

Mitch Omer, and his business partner, Steve Meyer, will tell you that they named their restaurant Hell's Kitchen because that is what it feels like amid the simmering pots, hot ovens, and bustle that comes with making food from scratch for a hungry crowd of customers. While Mitch and Steve have been known to be irreverent at times, they are pious when it comes to food.

Hell's Kitchen serves up creative and hearty breakfasts and lunches, which include things like ricotta-lemon pancakes and a walleye BLT. Mitch and Steve take good ingredients seriously and believe that homemade is always best. That is why not only is the food made from scratch, but so is the ketchup, mustard, marmalade, iced tea, tomato juice, and hot cocoa. Their homemade peanut butter won such rave reviews on National Public Radio's *Splendid Table* that they even had to start selling it online to keep up with demand.

It is not surprising that Mitch insists on the best-quality ingredients for the restaurant. Over the years, Mitch has developed relationships with a few local purveyors that, Mitch says, "I will

Mitch Omer and Steve Meyer

never leave." One of these is the Silver Bison Ranch in Baldwin, Wisconsin.

"I have been buying naturally fed and individually culled bison from Loren and Marilyn Smeester since long before I opened Hell's Kitchen," Mitch notes. After being reviewed in several magazines and newspapers about serving bison meat, Mitch says that every other bison rancher in a 500-mile radius wanted to sell to him. He explains, "But I have a personal relationship with this purveyor, this rancher, this friend. I will never buy bison from anyone else but them, and I will always have bison on my menus."

Another favorite ingredient that Hell's Kitchen buys direct is hand-harvested, wood-parched wild rice. They buy this exclusively from the Leech Lake Band of Ojibwe. "There is no other product, anywhere, that compares with this," he says. He uses the wild rice for his Mahnomin Porridge, which is an adaptation of a journal entry he first read about years ago while studying the writings of fur trappers from the 1800s. He explains, "It was recorded that French trappers observed northern Indians eating a meal of cooked wild rice with nuts, berries, and maple syrup." Mitch played around with those ingredients and finally perfected his recipe by adding heavy cream.

"When we first opened, no one would order the porridge," says Mitch. "It just seemed so foreign." But he was determined not to drop the item from the menu and began giving away samples for customers to try. His strategy worked. Mitch says, "I used to buy fifty pounds of wild rice every two or three months. Now I buy nearly fifty pounds a week to keep up with demand." The recipe for the Mahnomen porridge is one that is most requested by customers.

Using local foods is not a religion at Hell's Kitchen, but when they find the right local purveyor — it's a match made in heaven. As Mitch says about his bison and wild rice suppliers, "I'm practically married to these guys!"

MAPLE-GLAZED BISON SAUSAGE

This slightly spicy, maple syrup–sweetened sausage is the perfect accompaniment to a Hell's Kitchen breakfast, and a key ingredient in the restaurant's sausage bread. As the raw patty is charcoal-grilled, the maple syrup caramelizes on the outside, sealing in the natural juices and preserving the flavor of this wonderful meat.

Makes approximately eight 3-oz. patties

1 lb. ground bison
$\frac{1}{4}$ cup minced shallots
$\frac{1}{4}$ cup pure maple syrup
2 tablespoons minced garlic
2 teaspoons ground sage
2 teaspoons red pepper flakes
2 teaspoons fennel seed
1 teaspoon dried thyme
1 teaspoon ground white pepper
1 teaspoon kosher salt

Place all ingredients in a mixer fitted with a paddle and slowly blend together until just mixed. Do not over-mix the ingredients because this will compact the sausage and make for a tougher, drier product. With moist hands, patty the sausage mixture into 3-oz. portions.

Bison meat is so low in fat that these patties should be cooked no longer than 4 minutes per side. If charcoal broiling, you should cook the patties over a medium-high heat on a rack set 4 inches from the hot coals. For stovetop cooking, use a heavy skillet lightly oiled, and preferably cast iron. These sausage patties should cook over high heat.

Cook the sausages about 4 minutes per side. As mentioned earlier, Hell's Kitchen chefs cook their sausages over a charcoal grill. However, sautéing them in a skillet produces a juicier sausage because the patties cook in their own juices, instead of those juices dripping away through a grill grate. And never press down with a spatula on the sausages while they cook, since this pushes the flavorful juices out of the patties.

MAHNOMIN PORRIDGE

When Mitch Omer and Steve Meyer first opened Hell's Kitchen in 2002, they couldn't give this away. Yet Mitch so loved this porridge, he refused to give up on it and decided to give away tiny samples of it in espresso cups. Now word has spread like wildfire, and this porridge is one of Hell's Kitchen's top sellers.

Serves 4

4 cups cooked wild rice
$\frac{1}{2}$ cup roasted, cracked hazelnuts
$\frac{1}{4}$ cup sweetened dried cranberries (Craisens)
$\frac{1}{4}$ cup dried blueberries
$\frac{1}{4}$ cup pure maple syrup
1 cup heavy whipping cream

In a heavy, non-stick saucepan, add the cooked wild rice, hazelnuts, blueberries, Craisens, and maple syrup and cook over medium-high heat, about 3 minutes. Add the heavy cream and, stirring constantly, heat through, about 2 minutes. Ladle into bowls and serve immediately.

BISON SAUSAGE BREAD

This is a batter bread, rich and dense, and utilizing one of Mitch Omer's favorite foods in the world, bison. People might find it an odd recipe, using ground meat and coffee, but Mitch guarantees, once people try this, they will be hooked forever. This is best eaten browned in a toaster or grilled, and slathered in sweet cream butter. This is a meal unto itself.

Makes 1 loaf

10 oz. maple-glazed bison sausage; Italian sausage can be substituted
¾ cup dried blueberries
¾ cup dark roast prepared coffee
4 large eggs
¾ cup walnut pieces, toasted
¾ cup granulated sugar
½ lb. dark brown sugar
2 cups all-purpose flour
1 teaspoon baking powder
1 teaspoon baking soda
1 teaspoon cinnamon
1 teaspoon ground ginger
¼ teaspoon nutmeg
⅛ teaspoon ground cloves

Preheat oven to 350°F. In the bowl of an electric mixer fitted with a paddle, add the sausage, dried blueberries, and coffee and mix together slowly until well blended. Slowly add the eggs, one at a time, while slowly mixing.

Stop the mixer and add the remaining ingredients. Slowly beat together for 3 to 4 minutes, or until well blended. Stop the mixer and with a rubber spatula, scrape the bottom and sides of the mixing bowl. Beat another 2 to 3 minutes on medium speed.

Butter and flour a 5x9-inch loaf pan. Scrape the batter into the pan and bake about 1½ hours on the center rack of the oven. Test for doneness. Allow the bread to rest for 10 minutes in the pan; remove to a cooling rack. When cooled to room temperature, wrap the bread and refrigerate or freeze.

To serve, cut into thick slices, butter, and grill on a flat pan; or toast and serve well-buttered.

LUCIA'S RESTAURANT, LUCIA'S WINE BAR, AND LUCIA'S TO GO

Fischer Farm

While Lucia Watson is often referred to as the pioneer of the local food movement in Minnesota, she tends to think of herself more as going "back to the future." Lucia and her customers are moving out of the glitch we've been in since the post–World War II boom, when many people quit eating locally and healthfully. It's been a three-generation glitch!

A third-generation Minnesotan, Lucia's grandmother, Lucia Louise — "Lulu" — instilled the value of food in her. These days, Lucia is reminded of these traditions when she visits the farmers' markets in France. "When the market is in full swing, they still sell live rabbits, chickens, and pigeons, but only the older women are buying them," Lucia says. "When that generation goes, I don't think they'll be selling that way. That will be a sad day for a country that has always placed such value on their food and traditions."

While Lucia doesn't buy her chicken with the feathers on, she does buy the freshest ingredients she can find. Pork comes from Fischer Farms in Waseca. Vegetables come from Riverbend and other local farms.

Lucia has received many awards for her efforts to promote good local food. She is a board member of Youth Farm and

Lucia Watson

Market and an advocate of programs that teach youth about growing and cooking food. "When you see how differently kids approach food when they know more about it, it's just amazing," she says. "I taught a class where we were going to make peanut butter. The kids did not believe that it came from peanuts. That's such a symbol of how we've become disconnected between our food and where it comes from."

So what does Lucia suggest we do about it? "Consumers should expand their definition of local," she says. "If you randomly interviewed people, their ideas of local food are tomatoes, lettuce, and corn. The truth is, if you committed to buying all-local milk for one year, you would be making more of a difference in the local economy than going to the farmers' market every Saturday for the whole summer.

"Look at what's available locally. There's a lot in Minnesota — flour, butter, and wonderful cheese. Commit to getting a freezer; put twenty chickens, a quarter of a cow, a lamb in it. And then you have a really good local thing going, like my grandma Lulu. I just encourage people to take that first step."

BEER BATTER WALLEYE FINGERS WITH MAPLE-MUSTARD DIPPING SAUCE

The batter here is just a little bit different, an alternative to thinner mixes. Meanwhile, the simple maple-mustard dipping sauce is one of my all-time favorites. I use walleye to do this recipe, but any lean fish works just as well. Perhaps my overall favorite is perch.

Serves 1–2

½ cup flour
Salt and pepper to taste
¼ teaspoon baking powder
¼ teaspoon dry mustard
½ teaspoon cayenne powder
½ cup beer (room temperature)
Oil for frying
2 walleye fillets, bones removed, cut into fingers or appropriate portions

Combine the flour, salt, pepper, baking powder, mustard, and cayenne in a bowl. Add the beer and whisk. If you use cold beer, let the batter sit for an hour after mixing.

In a heavy pot, heat the oil to 350°F. Test the oil by sprinkling a few drops of batter into it. The batter droplets should sizzle and immediately rise to the top of the oil.

Dip the fish in the batter and thoroughly coat each fillet. Fry until crisp and golden, about 3 to 5 minutes. Remove with a slotted spoon and drain on paper towels.

MAPLE-MUSTARD DIPPING SAUCE
½ cup smooth Dijon mustard
3 tablespoons maple syrup

Mix together and taste for seasoning.

PORKETTA (GARLIC-FENNEL PORK ROAST)

Porketta is of Italian origin, but this garlic-studded, fennel-flavored, long-cooked roast has been adapted by everyone — Finn, Norwegian, and Cornish alike — who grew up on the Iron Range, the iron-mining area of northern Minnesota. Its very mention will elicit tender declarations from even the most stoic north woodsman.

This recipe was inspired by Margaret Erjavec of Virginia, Minnesota, who contributed it to *The Old Country Cookbook*. You may want to adjust the seasonings according to your own tastes. The meat must be cooked until it falls apart when touched with a fork. Porketta should not be sliced, but pulled apart. It is wonderful served with roasted potatoes at supper and is even better the next day or the day after, when eaten between slices of homemade bread.

Serves 8–10

1 boneless pork butt roast (6 pounds)
2 teaspoons salt
2 tablespoons freshly ground black pepper
10 cloves garlic, coarsely chopped
1 cup chopped fresh parsley
½ cup fennel seeds
¼ cup olive oil
1 large fennel bulb, finely chopped
6 new potatoes cut into large chunks
2 stalks celery, cut into chunks
6 carrots, cut into chunks
2 medium onions, peeled and cut into chunks

Cut the roast in half lengthwise and open it like a book. Combine all of the seasoning ingredients with the olive oil and rub it over both sides of the meat, pressing the fennel seeds and garlic into the meat. Spread the chopped fennel bulb over the meat, then fold the meat back together or roll it up and secure with a string. Place the meat in a roasting pan, cover, and bake in a preheated 325°F oven for 3 to 4 hours. Toward the last 30 minutes of cooking, scatter the vegetables on the bottom of the roasting pan and continue cooking the roast until it falls apart when touched with a fork.

Remove the roast from the pan and allow it to sit about 5 minutes before pulling it apart to serve with the vegetables.

CLASSIC ROSEWOOD INN
Alexis Bailly Vineyard

The town of Hastings, only twenty-five miles from downtown Saint Paul, lies at the juncture of the Mississippi, St. Croix, and Vermillion rivers. Like many northern river towns, Hastings is brimming with historic properties — sixty-two are listed on the National Register of Historic Sites.

Among these is the Classic Rosewood Bed and Breakfast, owned and run by Pam and Dick Thorsen. In 1983, Pam and Dick opened the Thorwood Inn, the first bed and breakfast in the state — making them the grandparents of the movement in Minnesota. The Thorwood Inn has recently been converted into three condos, one of which is Pam and Dick's home.

For Pam, running a bed and breakfast not only gives her the opportunity to meet interesting people from around the world — including Bob Newhart, Anthony Edwards, and even an English Lord — but also gives her an opportunity to be uniquely involved in her community. Pam offers her guests the option of signing up for "packages," which, in addition to a lovely room and breakfast, might also include dinner at a local restaurant, a in-suite massage from a local masseuse, or a tour (and bottle of wine) from nearby Alexis Bailly Vineyard.

Alexis Bailly is Minnesota's oldest winery, having opened in the late 1970s. It was the dream of David A. Bailly who,

Pam Thorsen

amid skeptics, set out to develop a fine Minnesota wine. On his death in 1990, David's daughter Nan took over the winery and has continued his legacy of making award-winning wines. From bold red wines, like Voyageur, to sweet ice wines, like Isis, Alexis Bailly has been a pioneer in Minnesota's growing wine industry.

Alexis Bailly is just one of the food gems in Pam's beloved St. Croix River Valley. When thinking of chocolatiers, Switzerland and Belgium often come to mind before Hastings and River Falls. But along the St. Croix, there are four chocolate makers who create unique and mouthwatering delicacies.

Building on these sweet assets in their communities, Pam and eleven other innkeepers — from Osceola and Taylors Falls in the north to Hastings and Prescott in the south — developed the Chocolate March. The event offers an array of chocolate-centered activities at the inns each Sunday during the month of March. Pam says, "It is a fun, tantalizing event. Guests get personalized tours of these historic inns and get to sample everything from truffles to chocolate chai tea."

A recent addition to the Chocolate March is the LeDuc Mansion in Hastings. The LeDuc Mansion was built in 1866 by William and Mary LeDuc. William was a Civil War quartermaster, the U.S. agricultural secretary under President Rutherford B. Hayes, and a pioneer horticulturalist.

When William became quartermaster, in charge of supplying and provisioning troops, he was outraged at the conditions under which the officers ate their meals. He ordered that tablecloths and china be used and that mealtimes be a cultured time. He also sought out fresh food for his troops, which was a challenge in wartime.

This interest in food and culture was reflected in the LeDuc estate, which included a large vegetable garden, an apple orchard, and a grape arbor. William was a horticultural entrepreneur. To develop apples that would withstand Minnesota winters, he imported apple and crab apple stock from Russian Siberia. He then crossbred these with domestic varieties. The LeDucs were influenced by Andrew Jackson Downing — the guru of taste at that time. His writings and how-to books influenced their house design and horticultural endeavors.

The house was given to the Minnesota Historical Society in 1958 but it wasn't open to the public until 2005. The old glory of the house and grounds are stunning, and staff and volunteers give tours and tell stories of the LeDuc family. The LeDuc staff have developed a series of interesting and inviting programs that build on the history of the LeDuc family and their love of food and agriculture. These include teas, brunches, and heritage food demonstrations. The grounds are also home to a farmers' market.

It is not surprising that Pam Thorsen sits on the board of the Dakota County Historical Society that oversees the LeDuc estate. It is another way to nurture the unique and interesting aspects of her community.

Nan Bailly

CURRIED CHUTNEY SPREAD ON CRISP APPLE SLICES

This spread is also nice in split organic dates or on toast points. We get our apples from Carpenter Nature Center.

Serves 3–4

8 oz. cream cheese, at room temperature

2 tablespoons milk

1 generous teaspoon Indian-style curry paste

2 heaping tablespoons Apple Cranberry Chutney (recipe follows)

½ cup pecan halves, toasted and coarsely chopped

2 large, crisp, red-skinned apples

1 tablespoon fresh lemon juice

Combine the cream cheese, milk, and curry paste in a mixing bowl. Working with the back of a spoon, blend until smooth. Stir in chutney, breaking up any excessively large pieces, and ¼ cup of the pecans (reserving the remaining for garnish).

Cut the apples into even quarters, remove the core, and cut each quarter into four lengthwise slices. Drop into a small bowl, add cold water to cover, and stir in lemon juice. Cover and refrigerate. When ready to serve, drain the apples and pat dry. Smear about 1 teaspoon of Curried Chutney Spread onto each apple slice, garnish with remaining pecans, and serve immediately.

Classic Rosewood Inn

ROASTED GREEN BEANS WITH SUN-DRIED TOMATOES, GOAT CHEESE, AND OLIVES

1 lb. green beans
1 tablespoon olive oil
1 teaspoon extra virgin olive oil
1 tablespoon lemon juice
1/2 cup oil-packed sun-dried tomatoes, drained
1/2 cup pitted kalamata olives
2 teaspoons minced fresh oregano leaves
1/2 cup crumbled goat cheese (about 2 oz.)

Adjust oven rack to middle position and heat oven to 450°F. Line rimmed baking sheet with aluminum foil; spread beans on baking sheet. Drizzle with oil, tossing by hand to coat evenly. Sprinkle with 1/2 teaspoon salt, toss to coat, and distribute in an even layer. Roast 10 minutes.

Remove baking sheet from oven. Using tongs, redistribute beans. Continue roasting until beans are dark golden brown in spots and have started to shrivel (10 to 12 minutes longer).

While beans roast, rinse, pat dry, and coarsely chop sun-dried tomatoes. Combine with extra virgin olive oil, lemon juice, olives (quartered lengthwise), and oregano in medium bowl. Add beans; toss well to combine. Add salt and pepper to taste. Transfer to serving dish and top with crumbed goat cheese.

WILD RICE–ZUCCHINI PANCAKES

Not just for breakfast! We serve these at our teas as one of the savory sandwiches; use sour cream as the butter between two 3-inch pancakes. They also make a wonderful appetizer.

1/2 pound zucchini, coarsely chopped
1 1/2 cups cooked wild rice
1 clove garlic
2 teaspoons lemon zest, grated
2 tablespoons fresh basil, chopped
1/2 teaspoon salt
2 eggs, beaten
2 tablespoons flour

1 tablespoon olive oil
Grated Parmesan cheese

Place zucchini in several thicknesses of paper towels; squeeze out excess moisture. In a bowl, combine zucchini with next seven ingredients. In a large non-stick griddle or skillet, heat 1/2 tablespoon oil over medium heat. Spoon heaping tablespoons of batter into skillet, about 4 inches apart, flattening each to form 3-inch pancakes. Cook, turning once, until golden brown, for about 15 minutes on each side. Transfer to plate and keep warm. With remaining oil and batter, cook remaining pancakes. Sprinkle with Parmesan cheese.

APPLE CRANBERRY CHUTNEY

Yield: 3 1/4 cups

2 cups peeled, chopped apples
1 cup fresh cranberries
1/4 cup golden raisins
2 tablespoons brown sugar
1 tablespoon grated orange rind
2 tablespoons cider vinegar
1/4 teaspoon ground cloves

1/4 teaspoon ground nutmeg
1/4 teaspoon ground cinnamon

Combine all ingredients in a non-aluminum saucepan. Place over high heat. Bring to a boil, stirring constantly. Reduce heat and simmer, uncovered, 15 minutes or until apples are tender. Remove from heat and let cool. With knife blade in processor, add mixture. Process, pulsing 1 or 2 times until combined. Place in a medium bowl. Cover and chill.

MINNESOTA LANDSCAPE ARBORETUM AND GOOD LIFE CATERING

The minute you start talking to Jenny Breen you know that she is an educator. Not a preacher, an educator. She bubbles over with information that is passed on in her cooking classes at the Minnesota Landscape Arboretum and through her style of catering in her company, Good Life Catering.

"I love teaching people to cook. It gives me an opportunity to connect, to share the love and joy of cooking, and the pleasure of eating good food and being a responsible consumer. . . . I love to show that to people," says Jenny.

The Arboretum is a perfect fit for Jenny's philosophy of food. In recent years, the Arboretum has worked to educate people about where food comes from and now is focusing on local food products and the people behind them.

"Food that is grown by local farmers just tastes better," is Jenny's mantra. "And, even if your taste buds aren't telling you that, why not put your money behind sustainably grown food?" she adds. "Some of our palates may need to be retrained. We're not accustomed to the leaner taste of grass-fed beef, but no one can tell me that a freshly picked Minnesota-grown carrot isn't candy sweet."

Jenny Breen

That joy of biting into a freshly picked vegetable is something that Jenny loves to share with children. At the Arboretum's kids cooking classes, young cooks pick items from a garden outside the door of the cooking classroom and then prepare their meal. "You'll rarely find a kid that doesn't like green beans that they've picked or grown themselves," Jenny says. All food comes from plants, one way or another. The Arboretum and Jenny teach that.

Jenny and the Arboretum are launching a new venture with Green Routes to bring people even closer to their food. Together they will offer culinary tours where participants will visit farms, wineries, and artisan food-makers and then use the bounty they collect to make a meal together, with Jenny's help.

While not a big-time gardener herself, Jenny is a firm believer in preserving the summer and fall bounty for use the rest of the year. Her freezer is full of soups, tomatoes, pesto, and other vegetables. "Freeze or can your food, the way people have done for years," she recommends. "Think ahead and be intentional in your eating. Intentionality around eating is the basis for it all. You have to get back to connecting with your food," she adds.

GRILLED GOUDA SANDWICH WITH ROASTED BEETS AND ARUGULA

Serves 6 as a meal, 12 as an appetizer

1 loaf hearty whole grain bread, sliced thin (enough for 6 full sandwiches, 12 appetizer portions if cut in half)
1/4 lb. unsalted butter
1 lb. Eichten, Pastureland, or Gouda cheese of your choice, sliced thin; smoked Gouda works well also
4 medium beets, peeled and sliced thin lengthwise
1/4 cup olive oil
1/4 cup balsamic vinegar
1 teaspoon salt
1/2 lb. arugula
Stone-ground mustard

Heat oven to 400°F. Cover beets in olive oil, balsamic vinegar, and salt, and roast in oven, stirring occasionally. Meanwhile, brush outsides of bread with butter, and insides with mustard. When beets are nicely tender, about 30 minutes, remove from oven. Remove from pan and reserve remaining liquid. Assemble sandwiches with a layer of arugula, a layer of beets, and a few slices of cheese over the top. To melt cheese, place open-faced sandwiches on baking pan and place in oven or in covered pan on medium heat. Remove when cheese is melted (about 1 minute). Drizzle with reserved oil and vinegar mixture from beets.

THREE SISTERS SALAD

Serves 6

2 cups pearled barley, cooked in 4 cups water
1/2 cup water
2 cups corn kernels (frozen or fresh off the cob)
1 lb. green beans, trimmed and cut into 2-inch pieces
1 small red onion, sliced thin
1 red bell pepper, sliced
1 cup dried tomatoes, sliced and re-hydrated in hot water
1 lb. cleaned, trimmed mustard leaves, baby spinach leaves, or other greens

Cook barley until tender; set aside. Heat water and steam corn and green beans until bright, about 2 minutes. Cool immediately under cold water. Combine barley with all vegetables and greens.

DRESSING
1/2 cup olive oil
1/4 cup cider vinegar
1/4 cup raspberry vinegar
2 tablespoons stone-ground mustard
2 tablespoons honey
1/4 cup fresh dill, chopped
4 cloves garlic, minced
2 teaspoons salt

Prepare dressing by combining all ingredients and whisking well. Pour half of dressing over salad mixture and add more according to taste.

CAFE BRENDA AND SPOONRIVER RESTAURANT

Mill City Farmers' Market

While still in her teens, Brenda Langton worked at the co-op vegetarian restaurant Commonplace in Saint Paul. At the age of twenty, she ventured off to Europe for a year, where markets, restaurants, and cooking with the local ingredients are a way of life. When she returned, she opened Cafe Kardamena in Saint Paul, a gourmet vegetarian and seafood restaurant.

A few years later, Brenda visited the Greens Restaurant in San Francisco. "Greens served beautiful vegetarian food that was grown on their own farm," she reminisces. Brenda was inspired and left with the idea of starting a restaurant in Minnesota that also sourced ingredients from local farmers. The day after her return from San Francisco, Brenda was touring downtown Minneapolis with some New York friends and discovered a brightly lit open space for lease in the warehouse district; that space became the home of Café Brenda.

"We've been a part of the community for nearly thirty years," says Brenda. "My commitment to eating healthy, natural food is just about feeling good and keeping our bodies and

Brenda Langton

minds healthy. I think the best way to teach people is by letting them eat whole grains, beans, seasonal vegetables, farm-fresh chicken, and responsibly harvested seafood. We now offer grass-fed beef, so we're not strictly vegetarian and haven't been for years, but people still tend to think of us that way."

Brenda's expansion with a second restaurant, Spoonriver, near the new Guthrie created yet another unexpected venture — the Mill City Farmers' Market. Brenda had planned to start a small farmers' market on the plaza next to Spoonriver when the building manager suggested she take a look at the train shed instead. Brenda realized it would be the perfect place. Mill City Farmers' Market became an overnight success, with more than forty-five local vendors providing fresh and flavorful food.

"With the market, I think people understand more of who I am and what I believe in," says Brenda. "We get people in from all over. They want to understand where their food comes from and to learn more about things like CSAs [community-supported agriculture]. Did you know we have more CSAs in Minnesota than any other state? How cool is that?"

With a CSA, a person or family buys a "share" from a local farm. Then they get a box of freshly harvested, locally grown food (usually vegetables, but sometimes eggs, flowers, honey, and so on) each week during the growing season. The variety of produce changes with the season, and customers share the risk with the farmer.

"CSAs are a great way to learn to cook with what you have," Brenda explains. "One week you'll get strawberries and asparagus; later in the year, tomatoes and squash. It forces you to think outside of the grocery-store-box mindset. Cook as simply as you can. Braise your greens with a little olive oil and goat cheese. Embrace Asian and Mediterranean styles of cooking, or simple Italian noodles. . . . That's comfort food. It's easy on digestion and delicious. Everything in moderation, even meat!"

EAST INDIAN POTATO AND PEA PASTRIES

Makes 10

FILLING

4 potatoes, medium cut into 1- to 2-inch chunks; this should equal 4 to 5 cups

1 tablespoon olive oil

2 teaspoons coriander seeds

¾ cup onion, diced

2 jalepeño or serano chilies, minced

1½ teaspoons grated fresh ginger (or 1 teaspoon dried)

1 cup frozen peas, thawed

2 teaspoons salt

1¼ teaspoons garam masala

1 tablespoon lemon juice

Cook potatoes in water for about 8 minutes, until soft. Drain, mash, cover, and set aside.

In a sauté pan, heat olive oil, add coriander seeds, and heat for about 15 seconds; they will turn dark brown. Add onions, chilies, and ginger, and continue to cook 4 to 5 minutes. Add garam masala, salt, and lemon juice. In a bowl, mix all filling ingredients.

PASTRY

4 tablespoons browned butter and 3 tablespoons vegetable oil, combined

1 package phyllo dough (10 sheets)

To prepare the pastries, heat oven to 400°F. Place 2 sheets of phyllo dough on countertop, vertically. Lightly brush with butter-oil mixture and cover with another sheet of phyllo. Cut the phyllo in half, place about ½ cup of filling mixture on each half of dough, and roll into a triangle. Continue with remaining phyllo and filling to make 10 pastries.

Bake at 400°F for 25 minutes, until golden brown.

VEGGIE BURGERS

2 tablespoons olive oil

5 ribs celery, minced

2 large onions, minced

3 large carrots, minced

2 heads garlic, minced

3 cups peanuts, roasted and coarsely chopped

3 cups sesame seeds, roasted and finely ground

3 cups sunflower seeds, roasted and coarsely chopped

2 cans navy beans, puréed separately

3 teaspoons mixed fresh or dried herbs (such as sage, basil, thyme)

Ancho chili powder

Black pepper, ground

8 cups cooked brown rice, blended until sticky; or 4 cups rice cooked in 7 cups water, blended until sticky

⅓ cup tamari

4 tablespoons tomato paste

2 tablespoons paprika

2 tablespoons fresh herbs, chopped

Salt to taste

6 to 8 eggs

1 to 2 cups matzo meal

Sauté minced vegetables in olive oil. Thoroughly mix vegetables with remaining ingredients, except eggs and matzo flour. Divide mixture into sixths or eighths, place into plastic bags, and freeze.

After thawing an individual bag of mixture, blend in one beaten egg and ¼ cup of matzo meal. Form mixture into three 4-oz. patties. Grill or fry.

TROTTER'S CAFÉ AND BAKERY

Northwoods Organic Produce

Local, fresh, and flavorful pretty much describe the basics of Saint Paul's Trotter's Cafe, but if you add community involvement, sustainable practices in all they do, and philanthropy, you'll be closer to the total Trotter's concept.

For almost twenty years, Dick and Pat Trotter's plan has been to buy local. The Saint Paul Farmers' Market, Whole Farm Co-op, Peace Coffee, Nowak Dairy, and Northwoods Organic Produce are some of the producers who have provided the bulk of the food that goes into the soups, entrees, scones, bread, and cookies that are all made "from scratch" on a daily basis. Stocks are simmered, chickens are poached, and bread is proofed for a menu that changes weekly, always incorporating what's seasonal.

"In an urban environment, we feel it's very important to have a rural connection," Dick says. "By supporting local growers we can help them continue, and they help us to give our customers flavorful, fresh products. We feel good knowing who grows the food we use and where it comes from; we can put a name or a face with many of the ingredients we use."

One of those faces is Dave Massey's of Northwoods Organic Produce. Dave, who farms near Pequot Lakes, is a chemist who worked with glues and adhesives for three decades

Pat and Dick Trotter

before retiring from Saint Paul–based H. B. Fuller. Ultimately, he combined his skill for problem-solving with his longtime passion for organic gardening and now raises extraordinary vegetables, berries, and seeds.

Dave won't claim he spent his career thinking outside the box. "I was always on the outer margins of the box, though," he says. With that in mind, it's not surprising that everything he does on his farm diverges somewhat from the typical center-of-the-box organic farmer. Only a farmer-chemist-troubleshooter would precisely measure the sugar content in his squash.

"I have a Ukrainian squash variety that is the sweetest squash you can find," Dave claims. "I even had the sugar tested. Nobody else has that variety." Dave has multiplied his Ukrainian squash seeds, which he obtained years ago from the Seed Savers Exchange in Decorah, Iowa, to the point where he can grow it commercially. But even so, demand is so high he can't keep up.

Dick and Pat like working with producers like Dave who are passionate about what they do. And with the variety of products Dave and others provide, Dick and Pat can create many options for their diners. "We have many vegetarian dishes. I think the variety helps the customer venture out into trying something different, like checking out a new soup flavor and complementing it with a favorite bread. There's always a new combination to try," Pat says.

She adds, "Food brings people together. Our business has changed a lot over the years, and always for the better. We listen to our customers. You gauge your business by the 'regulars.'"

And the regulars know that if you tip for good service, good things will happen. The employees decided years ago to donate the majority of their tip money to local charities. Every week, Trotter's also donates food to a local food shelf and an area shelter. If you bring in your own to-go container, you'll save a tree *and* save five percent on your purchase. A different local artist's work can be seen on the walls each month. Community meetings are welcome at this neighborhood cafe.

Dick says, "We feel there are so many things you can do to make a difference." And they do.

Dave Massey

TRIPLE FRUIT SCONES

Makes 12 scones

3 cups organic white flour
⅓ cup sugar
1 tablespoon baking powder
½ teaspoon baking soda
¼ teaspoon salt
3 oz. butter, cut into small pieces
⅓ cup chopped dried apricots
⅓ cup Craisins
1 egg
1 egg white
¾ cup buttermilk
2 teaspoons orange rind

Combine flour, sugar, soda, baking powder, and salt in mixing bowl. Add the butter, apricots, and Craisens; mix until butter is in pea-size pieces.

In a separate bowl, combine egg and egg whites, buttermilk, and orange rind. Add this liquid to the dry ingredients and mix until it just comes together. Using your hands, knead several times in bowl and then place the dough on a lightly floured board. Form dough into a 12x6-inch rectangle. Cut into 12 triangular pieces. Bake on a cookie sheet at 350°F for 13 to 16 minutes, or until lightly browned.

CARROT DILL SOUP

This soup is best when made with early small and sweet carrots. Makes a delicious chilled summer soup too!

12 medium carrots, peeled and cut into 3-inch pieces
Half of a medium onion, diced small
½ cup unsalted butter
½ cup fresh dill, minced
1 to 2 cups 2% milk
Salt and pepper to taste

Sauté the onions and carrots in butter for 10 minutes. Add the fresh dill and cook for 5 more minutes. Cover carrots with water and simmer until carrots are tender. Process carrots and liquid until smooth (use either an immersion blender or purée in batches in an upright blender) and return to pan. Add milk until soup is the consistency of a cream soup. Season with salt and pepper.

ZESTY CORNBREAD

This is a wonderful moist cornbread that can be as zesty as you'd like to make it.

Makes one 9x9-inch loaf

2 eggs
1 cup buttermilk
¼ cup canola oil
⅓ cup honey
1 cup white flour
1 cup corn meal
1 tablespoon baking powder
½ teaspoon salt

Optional add-ins:
½ cup fresh or frozen corn
¼ cup fresh or canned green chilies
2 tablespoons chopped hydrated sun-dried tomatoes
½ cup shredded cheddar cheese

Preheat oven to 350°F. Grease a 9x9-inch square or 9-inch round pan.

Whisk together eggs, oil, honey, and buttermilk. Set aside. Combine flour, corn meal, baking powder, and salt. Blend together. Add wet ingredients to the dry mix. Stir to combine. Fold in optional ingredients.

Pour batter into greased pan and smooth the surface. Bake for 25 to 30 minutes. Serve with Minnesota syrup and butter, or honey butter.

SWEET POTATO OAT CURRANT BREAD

Makes 2 loaves

2 tablespoons yeast
1¼ cups warm water
1¼ cup puréed sweet potato (recipe below)
¼ cup molasses
½ tablespoon salt
1 cup oats, Minnesota organic
1 cup currants
4½ cups white flour, organic
1 cup whole wheat flour, organic
1 egg white

Dissolve yeast in 100 to 110°F warm water; allow to activate. Add sweet potatoes, molasses, and 1½ cups of white flour. Mix until smooth. Add salt, oats, and rest of flour. Knead for 5 minutes, then add currants, and knead for 7 minutes more.

Let rise until doubled, covered in a warm spot. Form into loaves (this dough is too soft for a free-form loaf; form into pan-size shaped loaves). Place into two 8x4½-inch greased loaf pans, cover, and let rise again until almost doubled in size. Brush the egg white on top of the loaves, sprinkle with oats, and bake at 350°F for 30 to 35 minutes.

PURÉED SWEET POTATOES

Make sure you put the sweet potatoes on a baking sheet; otherwise, they will ooze sweet, sticky juice all over your oven bottom.

Cut a small slit in 2 to 3 sweet potatoes and bake at 350°F until soft, 40 to 50 minutes. Cool to room temperature. Peel the sweet potatoes and process flesh in a food processor, fitted with a steel blade, until smooth.

ACKNOWLEDGMENTS

The Minnesota Homegrown Cookbook has been a few years in the making. Even before the ink was dry on our first book, *Renewing the Countryside — Minnesota*, Tim King mentioned the idea of identifying small cafes and restaurants where you could get a good meal made from scratch. Always one to take up a good idea, Christy James, on her extensive travels throughout Minnesota, began sending us information on the great little cafes and restaurants she came across.

This book really got its wings when the North Central Sustainable Agriculture Research and Education (SARE) program provided a grant to Renewing the Countryside and its partners to boost awareness of sustainably grown foods. North Central SARE has done a world of good for local food systems through its support and promotion of sustainable farming and ranching.

Support from the W. K. Kellogg Foundation was also critical in bringing this project to life. Their support enables Renewing the Countryside to take on projects that help inform the public about important issues in our food system and in rural communities.

A knowledgeable and talented team of people contributed to the making of this book. The editorial committee, comprising Mary Brocker, Tim King, Chuck Knierim, Brett Olson, Derric Pennington, Alice Tanghe, and myself, spent many hours concepting and creating the framework for this book.

Derric Pennington, Andi McDaniel, and Sarah Johnson did a great deal of research and preliminary interviews with cafes and restaurants. Their tenacious efforts laid the groundwork for this and other projects.

The stories were brought to life through the poetic writing of Tim King and Alice Tanghe. Tim — part poet, part activist, part farmer — fully understands the anticipation of receiving a seed catalogue mid-winter and the satisfaction of harvesting one's crops after a season of hard work. Alice is a "foodie" at heart with extensive experience in publishing. She is passionate about a good story and good food, and knows all the great places to eat in the Twin Cities.

Tony Schreck's beautiful photos make up the illustrative backbone of this book. He traveled many miles to take the photos of the food, chefs, farmers, and landscapes you see here. Tony is renowned in the local media scene for being able to deliver amazing images from fast and painless location photo shoots.

The stunning photography of Richard Hamilton Smith, John Connell, and Kristi Link Fernholz helped us capture the "sense of place" of the different regions featured. As natives to those places, they have a unique ability to capture feeling in a photo. To tell the story of fishing on Lake Superior, John agreed to set out on a boat with Harley Tofte in October. While the pictures show a serene and placid lake, anyone who lives on the north shore will tell you that October can bring white caps worthy of legend. And Kristi captured wonderful images from western Minnesota on unrealistic last-minute timelines.

Dave Holman came to Renewing the Countryside for a summer job straight out of college. He proved to be an accomplished photographer and shot several of the stories featured here. Sidney Brush, Robb Long, Karen Reed, Jodi Ohlsen Reed, Dave Hansen, and Alice Tanghe helped fill the gaps where we couldn't schedule photo shoots or the existing photos were too good to pass by.

This brings us to the food. While you'd think recipes from accomplished chefs wouldn't need to be tested, the reality is that most chefs don't work from recipes that most of us would understand. Most are artists and often work by feel. . . a little more salt here or five minutes longer there. So Alice Tanghe, Mary Broeker, and Brett Olson spent many hours deciphering, testing, and, when needed, adjusting recipes to serve a few people — rather than an entire restaurant. Many thanks to them for their time and talent, and to the lucky people who sampled the dishes they prepared.

As editors, Alice Tanghe and Stephanie Larson whipped all the text for this book into shape. In addition to writing, recipe testing, and editing, Alice did the coordination for the Twin Cities portion of this book.

As creative director, Brett Olson developed much of the structure, look, and feel for the book. He also coordinated the photography and shot a number of the photos.

We are extremely grateful to Garrison Keillor for writing the foreword for this book.

A number of other people contributed to different aspects of this project and we want to acknowledge and thank them. They include Margaret Schnieders, Lindsay Rehban, Beth Nelson, Helene Murray, JoAnne Berkenkamp, Colleen Tollefson, Mary Jo Forbord, Kent Gustafson, Paul Hugunin, Christy James, Marcia Neely, Terrance T. Nennich, Monica Siems, Courtney Tchida, Pam Thorsen, Cathy Twohig, Bill Wilcke, and Beth Munnich.

Thanks to the many folks across the state who sent in suggestions for restaurants, cafes, and bed and breakfasts to include in this book. We wish we could have included them all but had a limited amount of space. On our website you can find a link to a growing list of eateries that serve local food.

We also want to thank Michael Dregni and the folks at Voyageur Press—Dorothy Molstad, James Kegley, and all the rest and their parent company MBI Publishing. Michael saw the potential in telling the story of a sustainable food system though a cookbook right away and has proven to be a great partner in publishing this book. Through this partnership we believe that we will reach a broader audience and gain the attention that a project like this deserves.

Lastly, a very special thanks to all the sustainable farmers across the state who are growing lovely and tasty food while caring for the environment and their communities and to all the chefs and cooks who incorporate these ingredients into their menus.

They are our local food heroes!

Jan Joannides
Renewing the Countryside

RESTAURANT DIRECTORY

The Amboy Cottage Cafe
100 Maine Street East
Amboy, MN 56010
507.674.3123
www.amboycottagecafe.com

Angry Trout Cafe
P.O. Box 973
Grand Marais, MN 55604
218.387.1265
www.angrytroutcafe.com

Backroom Deli, The Good Food Store
1001 Sixth Street NW
Rochester, MN 55901
507.289.9061
www.backroomdeli.com

Bayport Cookery
328 Fifth Avenue North
Bayport, MN 55003
651.430.1066
www.bayportcookery.com

Birchwood Cafe
3311 East 25th Street
Minneapolis, MN 55406
612.722.4474
www.birchwoodcafe.com

Brewed Awakenings Coffeehouse
24 Northeast 4th Street
Grand Rapids, MN 55744
218.327.0724
www.brewedawakenings.biz

Bryant Lake Bowl
810 West Lake Street
Minneapolis, MN 55408
612.825.3737
www.bryantlakebowl.com

Cafe Brenda
300 1st Avenue North
Minneapolis, MN 55401
612.342.9230
www.cafebrenda.com

Caribou Grill
225 East Broadway
Hallock, MN 56728
218.843.3740
www.wiktel.com/menus/caribougrill/

Chez Jude
411 West Highway 61
Grand Marais, MN 55604
218.387.9113
www.chezjude.com

Classic Rosewood Inn
620 Ramsey Street
Hastings, MN 55033
651.437.3297
www.classicrosewood.com

Corner Table
Nicollet Avenue & 43rd Street W
Minneapolis, MN 55409
612.823.0011
www.cornertablerestaurant.com

Country Bed & Breakfast
17038 320th Street
Shafer, MN 55074
651.257.4773
www.countrybedandbreakfast.us

Dancing Winds Farmstay
6863 County 12 Boulevard
Kenyon, MN 55946
507.789.6606

The Ellery House Bed and Breakfast
28 South 21st Avenue East
Duluth, MN 55812
800.355.3794
www.elleryhouse.com

El Norteño Restaurant
4000 East Lake Street
Minneapolis, MN 55406
612.722.6808

Gardens of Salonica
19 5th Street Northeast
Minneapolis, MN 55413
612.378.0611
www.gardensofsalonica.com

Heartland
1806 St. Clair Avenue
Saint Paul, MN 55105
651.699.3536
www.heartlandrestaurant.com

Hell's Kitchen
89 South 10th Street
Minneapolis, MN 55403
612.332.4700
www.HellsKitchenInc.com

Java River Cafe
210 South 1st Street
Montevideo, MN 56265
320.269.7106
www.javarivercafe.com

Lucia's Restaurant
1432 West 31st Street
Minneapolis, MN 55408
612.825.1572
www.lucias.com

Minnesota Landscape Arboretum
3675 Arboretum Drive
Chaska, MN 55318
952.443.1422
www.arboretum.umn.edu

Minwanjige Café
607 Main Avenue
Callaway, MN 56521
218.983.3834

New Scenic Cafe
5461 North Shore Scenic Drive
Duluth, MN 55804
218.525.6274
www.sceniccafe.com

Nosh Restaurant & Bar
310½ South Washington St.
Lake City, MN 55041
651.345.2425
www.noshrestaurant.com

Prairie Bay Restaurant
15115 Edgewood Drive
Baxter, MN 56425
218.824.6444
www.prairiebay.com

Restaurant Alma
528 University Avenue SE
Minneapolis, MN 55414
612.379.4909
www.restaurantalma.com

Scandinavian Inn
701 Kenilworth Avenue S
Lanesboro, MN 55949
507.467.4500
www.scandinavianinn.com

Saint Peter Food Co-op
119 West Broadway
Saint Peter, MN 56082
507.934.4880
www.stpeterfood.coop

Spoonriver Restaurant
750 South 2nd Street
Minneapolis, MN 55401
612.436.2236
www.spoonriverrestaurant.com

Trotter's Cafe
232 North Cleveland Ave.
Saint Paul, MN 55104
651.645.8950
www.trotters-stpaul.com

Writing Credits

Stories written by Tim King: Angry Trout Cafe — Dockside Fish Market; Chez Jude — Wild Acres; Ellery House Bed and Breakfast — Park Lake Farm; New Scenic Cafe — Bay Produce; Amboy Cottage Cafe — Whole Grain Milling Company; Java River Cafe — Dry Weather Creek Farm; Saint Peter Food Co-op — Shepherd's Way Farms; Caribou Grill — Double J Elk; Loghouse and Homestead on Spirit Lake — Muskrat Coffee Company; Minwanjige Cafe — Native Harvest; Nosh Restaurant & Bar — Rochester Farmers Market; Scandinavian Inn — Hilltop Acres Farm; The Backroom Deli — Dream Acres; Dancing Winds Farm Retreat — Callister Farm; Prairie Bay — The Farm on St. Mathias; Brewed Awakenings Coffeehouse — Spica Farm; Country Bed & Breakfast — Steve Anderson; Bayport Cookery — Thousand Hills Cattle Company

Stories written by Alice Tanghe: Restaurant Alma — Otter Creek Growers; Bryant Lake Bowl — Moonstone Farm; Birchwood Cafe — Riverbend Farm; Corner Table — Southeast Food Network; El Norteno — Whole Farm Co-op; Gardens of Salonica — Hill and Vale Farm; Heartland Contemporary Midwest Restaurant — Cedar Summit; Hell's Kitchen — Silver Bison Ranch; Lucia's — Fischer Farm; Minnesota Landscape Arboretum — Good Life Catering; Cafe Brenda and Spoonriver — Mill City Farmers' Market; Trotters Café and Bakery — Northwoods Organic Produce

Stories written by Jan Joannides: Classic Rosewood Inn — Alexis Bailey Vineyard

Photo Credits

Anthony Brett Schreck: page 2 top-left and bottom left and right, 6 right, 14, 15 left, 16, 18, 19, 20 left, 24, 25, 27, 29, 32, 33, 36, 39 bottom, 40, 41, 42, 43 right, 46, 47, 49, 50-51, 56, 58, 62, 65, 68, 70, 71, 73, 78, 79 left, 84, 86, 87, 89, 90, 92, 93, 96, 100, 101 bottom left and right, 103, 106, 107, 110, 111, 112, 113, 115, 116, 119, 121, 123, 124 top, 125, 130, 134, 135 bottom, 138, 148, 151, 152, 153.

Brett Olson: 1, 2 top-right, 5 left, 6 left, 7 right and left, 8, 9, 10, 20 right, 22 middle, 37, 39 top left, 52, 53, 54, 57, 59, 61, 63, 66-67, 69, 70 bottom right, 72, 77 top, 81, 82-83, 85 left, 91, 99, 101 top-left and right, 104, 105, 109, 122, 124 bottom, 126, 127, 128, 132, 133, 135 top, 142, 143, 149 bottom.

John Connelly: 11, 15 right, 34, 35.
Richard Hamilton Smith: 12, 13.
Kristi Link Fernholz: 74, 75 right, 76, 77 bottom.
David Hansen: 17.
David Holman: 22 top bottom, 44, 60, 75 left, 149 top.
Kris Hase: 30, 31.
Alice Tanghe: 146.
Karen Reed: 80 top right.
Jodi Ohlsen Reed: 79 right, 80 top left.
Sidney Brush: 97.
Robb Long: 80 bottom.

LOCAL FOOD RESOURCES

Minnesota has an amazing array of government, nonprofit, and for profit organizations working to strengthen and support the local food economy and bring great local foods to Minnesotans. Here is a partial list of resources related to local foods and sustainable agriculture.

Renewing the Countryside works to build a healthy food system by providing information and resources to eaters, farmers, food buyers, and others. Through events, publications, and online tools, RTC creatively brings the issues to life. RTC co-presents **Minnesota Cooks**, the **Healthy Local Foods** exhibit at the **EcoExperience**, and the **Homegrown Heartland** online marketplace for chefs, food buyers, and farmers. RTC also coordinates Green Routes.
Website: www.renewingthecountryside.org. Phone: 612.871.1541

Edible Twin Cities is a quarterly magazine that promotes the abundance of local foods in the Twin Cities area and surrounding communities. The magazine celebrates family farmers, chefs, food artisans, farmers' market vendors, and other food-related businesses committed to high-quality, seasonal, locally grown products.
Website: www.edibletwincities.net, Phone: 612.229.0498

Food Alliance Midwest, a program of **Cooperative Development Services** and the **Land Stewardship Project**, certifies farms and ranches that use sustainable agricultural practices. Visit the Food Alliance website to find a list of retail stores that carry Food Alliance certified products.
Website: www.foodalliance.org. Phone: 651.209.3382

Food Cooperatives (co-ops) are grocery stores that are owned by their members. Many co-ops carry a variety of local products, especially natural food cooperatives. Anyone can shop at a co-op and while a few maintain their "crunchy" stereotype, most are modern, full-service groceries. Minnesota has more than forty consumer food co-ops. Find locations, store names, and telephone numbers online at www.coopdirectory.org/directory.htm#Minnesota. Visit the Twin Cities Natural Food co-op website for farmer profiles and many great recipes.

Green Routes, an initiative run by **Renewing the Countryside**, helps people find one-of-a-kind places to eat throughout greater Minnesota. A website and glove box maps also identify unique places to play, shop, sleep, and learn — places where the owners are committed to using principles of sustainability in managing their enterprises.
Website: www.greenroutes.org. Phone: 612.871.1541

The Heartland Food Network, facilitated by the **Minnesota Project**, encourages the purchasing of local, sustainable, or organic foods. Restaurants and distributors who participate in the network actively support local farmers and communities by purchasing local foods. Choose restaurants that display the Heartland Food Network logo!
Website: www.heartlandfoodnetwork.org. Phone: 651.645.6159

The Homegrown Heartland Online Marketplace is a website that makes finding local foods easy for chefs, caterers, and institutional dining establishments. Local farmers, producers, and food distributors update the site regularly so food buyers know what is and will be available. The website is a joint project of the **Heartland Food Network** (a program of **Minnesota Project**) and **Renewing the Countryside**.

The Institute for Agriculture and Trade Policy, based in Minneapolis, advocates for policies and collaborates on projects that promote a healthy and local food system that strengthens agriculture's economic vitality. IATP works on issues of food and health, agriculture and the environment, and making local, sustainably grown foods available in low-income neighborhoods. ATP oversees the Sow the Seeds Fund that supports our local food system.
Website: www.iatp.org. Phone: 612.870.0453

Land Stewardship Project features two farmer directories: the **Stewardship Food Network** — a list of LSP farmer and retailer members marketing sustainably-produced vegetables, fruits grains, meats and dairy product — and its **Directory of CSA Farms** delivering to shareholders in the Twin Cities metro area. This website also provides links to numerous other farmer lists, organizations and resources that connect consumers to fresh, local foods.
Website: www.landstewardshipproject.org, Phone: 651.653.0618

The Minnesota Bed & Breakfast Association provides an online directory to great independent lodgings across the state. Choose anything from a Victorian mansion to a peaceful cottage in the woods, from a lakeside castle to a log house, from a former hospital to a former church. Many bed and breakfasts incorporate local ingredients into their menus. Ask about local foods when you make your reservation.
Website: www.minnesotabedandbreakfasts.org. Phone: 651.438.7499

The Minnesota Department of Agriculture's Sustainable Agriculture and **IPM Programs** provide farmers and consumers with information and programs on organic production practices, certification, market trends, and other topics.
Website: www.mda.state.mn.us/about/divisions/agdev.htm. Phone: 651.201.6012

Minnesota Cooks brings together well-known chefs, farmers, and celebrities to discuss and celebrate the great foods produced in Minnesota. Through events, an annual calendar, and a website, Minnesota Cooks shares stories of farmers and chefs, creative photography, recipes, and essays. Minnesota Cooks is presented by **Minnesota Farmers Union**, **Food Alliance Midwest**, and **Renewing the Countryside**.
Website: www.minnesotacooks.org. Phone: 651.639.1223

Minnesota Farmers Union is a nonprofit membership-based organization that works to protect and enhance the economic interests and quality of life of family farmers and ranchers and rural communities. MFU is the founder and co-presenter of **Minnesota Cooks** events and website.
Website: www.mfu.org. Phone: 651.639.1223

Minnesota Food Association works to build a more sustainable food system. MFA operates the **Agricultural Training Center** at Wilder Forest with the goal of relocalizing food systems. Programs include the **May Farm CSA**, the **New Immigrant Agriculture Project**, **Big River Foods** (a food distribution service), and a program that delivers fresh, local produce to area food shelves.
Website: www.mnfoodassociation.org, Phone: 651.433.3676

The Minnesota Grown Program is a statewide partnership between the **Minnesota Department of Agriculture** and Minnesotans who grow or raise specialty crops and livestock. The Minnesota Grown Program features a statewide directory of nearly 700 farmers, markets, and CSAs who market directly to consumers. Search online by product or location or request a free printed copy by mail.
Website: www.minnesotagrown.org. Phone: 651.201.6510

The Minnesota Institute for Sustainable Agriculture fosters connections between the sustainable agriculture community and the **University of Minnesota**. MISA's website includes links to local food directories, publications, and a calendar of events. Two recent publications include: *Local Food: Where to Find It, How to Buy It* (2005) and *Marketing Local Foods* (2007), a publication for farmers. Both are available at the MISA website.
Website: www.misa.umn.edu. Phone: 612.625-8235

The Sustainable Farming Association of Minnesota supports the development and enhancement of sustainable farming systems through innovation, demonstration, education, and farmer-to-farmer networking. Chapters are located throughout Minnesota and many include local directories of farms and products.
Website: www.sfa-mn.org. Phone: 866.760.8732

The UMN Regional Sustainable Development Partnerships create partnerships between communities and the **University of Minnesota** that encourage production and use of locally grown foods and the development of self-reliant regional systems that provide nutritious food, nurture healthy environments, and create economic opportunities for the people of Minnesota.
Website: www.regionalpartnerships.umn.edu. Phone: 612.625.8235 or 800.909.64720

If you can't find what you need here, feel free to contact us at **Renewing the Countryside**. Phone: 866.378.0587 or 612.871.1541. Email: info@rtcinfo.org

INDEX